THE ROBERT BURNS
INFORMATION
AND QUIZ BOOK

THE ROBERT BURNS
INFORMATION
AND QUIZ BOOK

by

HAROLD THOMAS

ALBYN PRESS

© Harold Thomas, 1988
Made and printed
in Great Britain
and published by
ALBYN PRESS
Whittingehame House
Haddington
East Lothian

ISBN 0284 98767 0

*Dedicated to
My Wife Ann, and
Daughter Dian*

SECTION 1

QUESTION 1
What rank did Burns' sons (a) James Glencairn Burns
(b) William Nicol Burns
attain in the East India Company?

Answer
(a) Lieut Colonel, 1855 (b) Colonel, 1855
Sir James Shaw, a relative of the Burns family, arranged the careers of these two sons of Burns. Both retired to Cheltenham and, on their deaths, were buried in the mausoleum, St Michael's Churchyard, Dumfries.

QUESTION 2
Which friend of Burns was descended from the Scottish patriot, Sir William Wallace?

Answer
Mrs Frances Dunlop of Dunlop who, recovering from her husband's death, chanced to read a copy of "The Cottar's Saturday Night". She immediately got in touch with the poet and started a long friendship. Whilst offended by some of Burns' ideas, she tried hard to help him, two of her suggestions being a commission in the Army, and the Professorship of Agriculture at Edinburgh University.

QUESTION 3
(a) Whom did Burns describe as "Meikle Ursa Major"?
(b) When and why?

Answer
(a) Dr Samuel Johnson
(b) The poem "The Fête Champêtre" refers to a social gathering of Ayrshire land owners and well-to-do residents as guests of Cunninghame of Enterkine and Annbank. James Boswell, the latter day diarist, was spoken of, hence the mention of Johnson whom Boswell "led o'er Scotland a'".

QUESTION 4
Who was Robert Burns' "Elder brother in misfortune"?

Answer
The poet Robert Fergusson, 1750-1774, a young Edinburgh poet who died, neglected, in a mad house. His work and use of local language greatly influenced Burns.

5

MRS FRANCES DUNLOP
OF DUNLOP
See Questions 2, 212

ROBERT BURNS
BY ALEXANDER NASMYTH
See Questions 112, 133, 258

COLONEL WILLIAM
NICOL BURNS
See Questions 1, 112, 258

WILLIAM SMELLIE
See Questions 36, 294

6

QUESTION 5
(a) Who was the chiel "amang us takin' notes"?
(b) From which poem/letter is this extract taken?

Answer
(a) Captain Francis Grose, the antiquarian friend of Burns. A former Army captain, he took up history and published several works.
(b) The quotation refers to his wise habit of note taking and the humorous poem refers to his abilities in the Army and as an antiquarian. The poem has the long title of "On the late Captain Grose's Peregrinations thro' Scotland". It was published in 1789.

QUESTION 6
To whom did Burns mention his philosophy that "If I could, and I believe I do as far as I can, I would wipe away all tears from all eyes"?

Answer
To Peter Hill, an Edinburgh bookseller, in a letter dated 2nd March, 1790.

QUESTION 7
"Curse Thou his basket and his store, Kail and potatoes. . ."
    Whose?

Answer
Gavin Hamilton who was a thorn in the flesh to the stern Calvinist preachers. "Holy Willie" Fisher in the hypocritical prayer seeks Holy judgement on lawyer Hamilton.

QUESTION 8
Who cancelled his subscription to the First Kilmarnock Edition and what did Burns call him?

Answer
William Lorrimer cancelled his copy and Burns wrote on the subscribers' sheet: "The blockhead refused it." Lorrimer might well have not been able to afford the three shillings cost of the poems so cancelled his order.

QUESTION 9
To whom did Burns write saying, "I am at this moment ready to hang myself for a young Edinburgh widow"?

Answer
Richard Brown.

Curse on ungrateful man, that can be pleas'd,
And yet can starve the author of the pleasure!

Mr Robert Fergusson
Ælıʀı, xxıv

O thou, my elder brother in Misfortune,
By far my elder Brother in the muse,
With tears I pity thy unhappy fate!
Why is the Bard unfitted for the world,
Yet has so keen a relish of its pleasures?

PORTRAIT OF ROBERT FERGUSSON
WITH INSCRIPTION BY BURNS
See Questions 4, 194
8

Brown, born in Irvine, Ayrshire met Burns in the autumn of 1781, when Burns was staying in Irvine learning flax dressing. The romantic figure of a dashing young seaman, who became the master of a West Indiaman, seems to have "fired" the poet's imagination and broadened his outlook on the opposite sex.

In a letter to Brown from Edinburgh on December 30th, 1787 Burns wrote, "Do you recollect a Sunday we spent in Eglinton Woods? You told me, on my repeating some verses to you, that you wondered I could resist the temptation of sending verses of such merit to a magazine. 'Twas actually this that gave me an idea of my own pieces which encouraged me to endeavour at the character of a poet."

QUESTION 10
Who were "The Belles of Mauchline"?

Answer
Miss Miller; Miss Markland; Miss Smith; Miss Betty; Miss Morton and Jean Armour.
(a) Miss Helen Miller married Burns' friend Dr Mackenzie.
(b) The "Divine" Miss Markland was married to Mr James Findlay, an excise officer first at Tarbolton and afterwards at Greenock.
(c) The "witty" Miss Jean Smith bestowed herself upon Mr James Candlish, who, like Findlay, was a friend of Burns.
(d) The "braw" Miss Betty Miller became Mrs Templeton; she was the sister of Miss Helen Miller, and died early in life.
(e) Miss Morton gave her "beauty and fortune" to Mr Paterson, a merchant in Mauchline.
(f) Of Armour's history immortality has taken charge.

QUESTION 11
Burns sent a copy of his "Address to Edinburgh" on to William Chalmers of Ayr 27th December 1786. He describes a certain lady in the following terms:
"There has not been anything nearly like her in all the combinations of beauty, grace and goodness the great Creator has formed, since Milton's Eve on the first way of her existence."
Who was the lady?

Answer
Elizabeth Burnett.

She was born in 1766, the youngest daughter of Lord Monboddo. After her death in 1790 from consumption, at Braid Farm near Edinburgh, she became the subject of his "Elegy on the late Miss Burnett of Monboddo". She is buried in Greyfriars Churchyard, Edinburgh.

9

CAPTAIN FRANCIS GROSE
See Questions 5, 111, 197, 293

QUESTION 12
Who was the model for Dr Hornbook?

Answer
John Wilson.

Burns wrote this poem early in 1785 though it was not published in the Kilmarnock Edition. John Wilson was a Tarbolton schoolmaster who, to eke out the scanty subsistence set up a grocery shop. Although having only a very limited knowledge of medicine, he undertook the sale of a few medicines and went so far as to advertise that medical advice would be given at the shop gratis.

QUESTION 13
Who was "Dear bought Bess"?

Answer
Elizabeth Burns.

She was Burns' first illegitimate daughter, born in 1784 to Elizabeth Paton, a servant girl in the Burns' household, and was baptized when only two days old.

When Burns was contemplating his journey to Jamaica in July 1786, it was arranged that his brother, Gilbert, would rear the child as one of his own until her fifteenth year, and he assigned all his moveable effects and any profits from his publications to him.

QUESTION 14
Who was "Johnie Pigeon"?

Answer
John Dove or Dow.

He was the innkeeper of the Whitefoord Arms at Mauchline, an inn frequented by Burns. Dow it is said, originally came from Paisley. Burns was a member of a bachelors club which, in 1758, held their meetings in the Whitefoord Arms.

QUESTION 15
Who, according to Gilbert Burns, was the heroine of the song "Sweet Afton"?

Answer
Mary Campbell.

This popular song first appeared in *The Scots Musical Museum* in 1792. Some are of the opinion that it was written in praise of Afton Water, and as a compliment to Mrs Stewart of Stair, who received a copy of the song from the poet in 1791.

11

QUESTION 16
Who was "Racer Jess"?

Answer

A half-witted daughter of the Gibsons of Poosie Nansie's in Mauchline.
"Racer Jess" was so called because of her remarkable speed when sent on an errand. Poosie Nansie's is still an inn.

QUESTION 17
Who was the prototype of "Souter Johnnie"?

Answer

John Davidson, the "Souter Johnnie" of the poem "Tam O'Shanter" was a shoemaker famous for "Jest and Smart Sayings", residing in Kirkoswald. The original house has been carefully preserved, and is open for inspection.

QUESTION 18
Burns wrote to Clarinda: "I thank you for going to Miers, I want it for a breast pin to wear next to my heart." Who was Miers?

Answer

John Miers was an artist specialising in the taking of silhouette portraits, and both Burns and Clarinda sat for him. Miers came from Leeds and spent two years of his life in Edinburgh from 1786 to 1788. Of his later life, little is known.

QUESTION 19
Who was married to James Thomson, a writer in Dumfries?

Answer

Jessy Lewars, who married him in 1799: they had five sons and two daughters. She died in 1855 and is buried in St Michael's Churchyard, close to Burns, in Dumfries.

She was the youngest daughter of John Lewars, supervisor of excise in Dumfries. After her father's death, she lived with her brother, John Lewars (junior), who was a brother exciseman of Burns.

Jessy lived in a house opposite Burns' home in Mill Vennel (now Burns Street) and she faithfully helped nurse the poet during the last six months of his illness, although only eighteen years old.

Near the end of his life, Burns penned "O wert thou in the cauld blast." Many believe this to be his last work, and dedicated to Jessy.

QUESTION 20
According to Gilbert Burns, where did Burns first hear the spinet played?

Answer
In the Edinburgh home of the Rev. Dr. George Lawrie, played by his daughter, Christina.

Christina, or Christie Lawrie, was born in 1766 and married Alexander Wilson, a Glasgow bookseller. On February 5th, 1787, Burns wrote to her father saying:

"By far the most agreeable hours I spend in Edinburgh must be placed to the account of Miss Lawrie and her pianoforte."

She died in 1827.

QUESTION 21
To whom was Burns referring, when he wrote, "If there's another world, he lives in bliss, If there is none, he made the best of this."

Answer
William Muir.

Muir was the owner of Willie's Mill in Tarbolton, mentioned in "Death and Dr Hornbook". He befriended Jean Armour, when she became pregnant for the second time, by affording her shelter in his home.

QUESTION 22
One of the "Mauchline Belles" unfortunately died giving birth to her first child. Who was she?

Answer
Betty Miller.

Betty was the daughter of John Miller, and sister of Helen Miller and married a Mauchline merchant, William Templeton. That lovely song "From thee, Eliza, I must go" was inspired by her, and appeared in the Kilmarnock Edition.

QUESTION 23
"O once I loved a bonnie lass."
Who was the lass?

Answer
Nellie Kilpatrick.

Claimed to be the first poem written by Burns, "Handsome Nell" was inspired by Nellie Kilpatrick, the daughter of a blacksmith near Mount Oliphant. She was the poet's partner in the harvest field in the autumn of 1773 when he was 14. Writing of it in his first Common Place Book, under the date August 1783, he says,

"I never had the least thought or inclination of turning poet till I got

WILLIE'S MILL, TARBOLTON
(*See Question 21*)

BURNS' MAUSOLEUM
DUMFRIES
See Questions 1, 29, 65

THE BUILDING IN WHICH THE
KILMARNOCK EDITION WAS PRINTED
See Questions 51, 77, 132, 231, 296

14

once heartily in love and then rhyme and song were, in a manner, the
spontaneous language of my heart. "

QUESTION 24
To whom was Burns referring when mentioned "My first poetic
patron" and my, "First kind patron"?

Answer
Robert Aiken.

Aiken was born in 1739, the son of an Ayr sea captain. He became a
prosperous lawyer in the town of Ayr, where he met Burns in 1783. He
collected the names of one hundred and forty five subscribers for the
Kilmarnock Edition of Burns poems, a quarter of the total.

Burns dedicated "The Cottar's Saturday Night" to Aiken, and
"Epistle To a Young Friend" to his son, Andrew Hunter Aiken. Burns
wrote many letters to Aiken, one dated 8th October, 1786, which
mentioned his first thoughts of becoming an excise officer.

QUESTION 25
To whom was Burns referring when he wrote "The only artist who has
hit genuine pastoral costume. "

Answer
David Allan.

Allan was born in 1744, and known as "The Scottish Hogarth." His
works include many illustrations of Burns and Allan Ramsay. His grave
in Old Carlton Cemetery is marked by a monument with a marble
medallion, erected to his memory in 1874 by the Royal Scottish
Academy.

QUESTION 26
To whom did Burns send the following poems; "The Lass of Ballochmyle", "My Nannie O", "The Handsome Nell", and "The Vision"?

Answer
Mrs Alexander Stewart of Stair.

In September 1786 the poet sent a parcel of poems known as the Stair
Manuscript to Mrs Alexander Stewart. In 1791 he prepared for her the
manuscript collection now in the Cottage Museum (Afton Manuscript).

QUESTION 27
Burns said, "She was not a beauty, but had many charming qualities,
heightened by an education. "

To whom was he referring?

Answer

Ellison (or Alison) Begbie.

It seems probable that Burns was inspired by Miss Begbie to write "On Cessnock Banks a Lassie Dwells."

QUESTION 28

According to Gilbert Burns, who made the following reference to the poet: "I attempted to teach them a little Church music. Robert's ear in particular was remarkable dull, and his voice untunable"?

Answer

John Murdoch.

Murdoch was born in Ayr in 1747, and, when only eighteen years old, was engaged by William Burnes to teach his children. When the Burnes family moved to Mount Oliphant Robert and Gilbert continued tuition for two years.

Unfortunately, Murdoch left the district, but returned in 1772, during which time Burns received further instruction. After teaching for some time in Dumfries, he became a teacher of the English language in Ayr and Robert was sent there to revise his English grammar with his former teacher, but was recalled after only one week to assist on the farm.

Murdoch's career at Ayr came to an abrupt end on 14th February, 1776. Thereafter, he went to London and taught French for a period. He died in poverty in 1824.

QUESTION 29

Where did Burns' eldest son Robert continue his education after leaving Dumfries Academy?

Answer

At Glasgow and Edinburgh universities. Robert Burns, jun. was born on 3rd September, 1786 and was only ten years old when his father died on 21st July, 1796. After leaving university, he took an appointment at Somerset House and remained there for thirty years. His wife was a Miss Anne Sherwood who, when living in Dumfries, occupied a house in English Street. Robert jun. died in May 1857 and is buried beside his father and wife in the Mausoleum in St Michael's Churchyard in Dumfries.

QUESTION 30

In the "Epistle to James Tennant" who was Wabster Charlie?

Answer

Charles Tennant.

16

But Pleasures are like poppies spread,
You sieze the flower, its bloom is shed;
Or like the snow falls in the river,
A moment white, then melts for ever;
Or like the Borealis' race,
That flit ere you can point their place;
Or like the rainbow's lovely form,
Evanishing amid the storm:
Nae man can tether Time or Tide,
The hour approaches Tam maun ride;
That hour, o' Night's black arch the key-stane,
That dreary hour Tam ~~takes~~ mounts his beast in;
And sic a night ~~Tam~~ he took the road in,
As ne'er poor sinner was abroad in. —

   The wind blew as 'twould blawn its last,
The rattling showers rose on the blast,
The speedy gleams the darkness swallowed,
Loud, deep, & lang, the thunder bellowed:
That night, a child might understand
The deil had business on his hand. —

   Weel mounted on his, grey meare, Meg,

A MANUSCRIPT PAGE OF TAM O'SHANTER

See Questions 31, 76, 85, 97, 122, 186, 189, 193, 205, 215, 293

Tennant was born in 1786 and was the fourth son of John Tennant of Glenconner. He went to learn weaving in Kilbarchan, started a bleaching business in Barrhead and obtained a patent for the manufacture of chloride of lime, later forming the company of Tennant Knox & Co, and building his works in St Rollox, Glasgow.

QUESTION 31

In "Tam O' Shanter" who was the miller who brought the load of corn?

Answer

Robert Niven.

Robert was the son of John Niven, sen. and father of John Niven, jun. and was the tennant of the mill and farm of Ballochneil near Kirkoswald.

"That ilka melder, wi' the miller,
Thou sat as lang as thou had sillier"

QUESTION 32

"Better a wee bush than nae bield"

This quote is familiar to us all in many forms, it is also on the gravestone of one of Burns' "lasses". Who was the lady?

Answer

Jean Lorimer (Chloris).

She was born in 1775 and is buried in Newington Burying Ground, East Preston Street. The monument consists of a Celtic cross of granite and amid the Celtic carvings is "Better a wee bush than nae bield." Jean was "Chloris" and the "Lass wi' the lint white locks." She died in 1831. The stone was erected under the auspices of the Ninety Burns Club, Edinburgh, in 1901.

QUESTION 33

Where would you find a memorial to "Clarinda"?

Answer

On the wall of Bristo School, Edinburgh. The home of "Clarinda" was located in the Potterrow, Edinburgh, but like many landmarks it has suffered obliteration in the march of progress and the site is now occupied by Bristo School.

A tablet in bronze has been fixed to the wall of Bristo School and the unveiling ceremony was performed by Mr John Trotter D.Sc., founder and first president of "Clarinda" Burns Club on the 22nd January, 1938. The tablet reads thus:

Near this spot resided "Clarinda"
Friend of Robert Burns 1787 1791

QUESTION 34

"Yon auld grey stane, among the heather, mark's out his head; Whare Burns has wrote, in rhyming blether, 'Tam Samson's dead'." Who was Tam Samson?

Answer

Samson was born in Kilmarnock in 1722. "A zealous sportsman, and a good fellow" he died in 1795 and is buried in the Laigh Kirkyard in Kilmarnock. Burns recalls an incident when Tam had been moor fowling and got the idea that it was to be the last time he would do so, and expressed a desire to be buried on the moors. This gave Burns the opportunity to write his "Elegy and Epitaph" – Tam Samson's Elegy. The meeting place of Burns and Samson was in the Bowling Green House, an inn kept by Samson's son-in-law, Alexander Patrick, and it was here, at a party, Burns read "Tam Samson's Elegy" to an assembled company.

QUESTION 35

One of the few surviving letters Burns wrote in his youth, was sent to a former classmate, when they attended Hugh Rodger's School at Kirkoswald.
   Who was he?

Answer

Thomas Orr.

   Thomas Orr was the son of Jean Robinson, herself the daughter of Julia Robinson (believed to have been a witch) of Park Farm near Kirkoswald. Whilst Burns was studying surveying at the school, Orr was studying navigation and went to sea and was believed drowned on his first voyage in 1785.

QUESTION 36

Who introduced Burns to the Crochallan Fencibles?

Answer

William Smellie.

   William Smellie was the printer Burns met in Edinburgh, via William Creech, and had his printing office at the foot of Anchor Close. It would appear that Smellie was the originator of the club in 1778, and it took its name from a Gaelic air "Chro Challin", the cattle of Colin, and the Fencible part of the title was a mock imitation of the Home Guard which came into being at the time of the American Civil War. The club met in Dawney Douglas' tavern, believed to have been used by Mary Queen of Scots as a council chamber.

19

QUESTION 37
Who was "Black Russell"?

Answer
The Rev. John Russell.
Burns was opposed to Russell due to his teachings and ranting and raving. Burns referred to him as "Black Russell" in the poem "The Holy Fair". He also appears as "Rumble John" in "The Kirk's Alarm and in "The Twa Herds". He died in 1817.

QUESTION 38
Who, when visiting Burns at Brow on the 15th July, 1796 where the poet was undergoing his "Medical Treatment", was horrified at the deterioration in his health and appearance?

Answer
John Syme.
John Syme was the son of the Laird of Barncailzie in Kirkcudbrightshire and like his father was a Writer to the Signet. Before retiring to his father's estate he spent some years in the army. He moved to Dumfries in 1791, with an appointment to the sinecure of Collector of Stamps for the district, with an office on the ground floor of a house in what is now Bank Street. In 1794, he accompanied Burns on his summer tour through Galloway. Syme and Dr Maxwell arranged the poet's funeral and along with Alexander Cunningham raised money to help Burns' widow and children.

QUESTION 39
"Mony a laugh, and mony a drink,
And aye eneugh o' needfu' clink.
To whom did Burns address this?

Answer
James Tennant.
James, the eldest son of John Tennant of Glenconner, was born in 1755 and was known locally as "The Miller" owing to the fact that he was the owner of a mill in Ochiltree. He was also Burns' "Auld comrade dear and brither sinner." He died in 1835.

QUESTION 40
Burns wrote to a friend round about the time he was contemplating his journey to Jamaica. "I am going perhaps to try a second edition of my book. If I do, it will detain me a little longer in the country. If not, I shall be gone as soon as harvest is over."
    To whom was Burns writing?

Answer
John Richmond.
   John Richmond was born in Sorn in 1765 and became a clerk in Gavin Hamilton's office, where Burns met him. It was Richmond who told of Burns' drunken race on horseback along the side of Loch Lomond with a wild Highlandman, resulting in a "skinful of bruises and wounds" for the poet. When Burns first arrived in Edinburgh he shared both room and bed with Richmond in the flat of Mrs Carfrae in Baxter's Close, Lawnmarket.

QUESTION 41
Who maintained that she was the Annie of "The Rigs o' Barley"?

Answer
Ann Rankine.
   Ann, the youngest daughter of John Rankine of Adamhill Farm, married John Merry, an innkeeper in Cumnock.
   She died in 1843 and is buried in Cumnock old Churchyard.

QUESTION 42
Who is the Meg in the "First Epistle to Davie"?

Answer
Margaret Orr.
   Margaret was a servant of Mrs Stewart of Stair House. She became the wife of John Paton and was not, as is sometimes claimed, the wife of David Sillar.

QUESTION 43
Who was "The Bonnie Lass of Ballochmyle"?

Answer
Miss Wilhelmina Alexander. Written in 1786, this widely esteemed song was inspired by Miss Alexander, the sister of Mr Claud Alexander, who had shortly before succeeded the Whitefoords as proprietor of Ballochmyle estate. On the 19th November of that year, the enclosed verses, in a letter to Miss Alexander, read,
   "I have roved about, as chance directed, in the favourite haunts of my muse on the Banks of Ayr, to view nature in all the gaiety of the vernal year. It was a golden moment for a poetic heart. Such was the scene, and such was the hour, when in the corner of my prospect I spied one of the fairest pieces of nature's workmanship that ever crowned the poetic landscape, or met a poet's eye."
Much to the mortification of Burns, the lady took no notice.

21

QUESTION 44

"Agitated, hurried to death, I sit down to write a few lines to you, my dear, dear, friend."
From whom did Burns receive this letter?

Answer

Clarinda.

Clarinda, Mrs McLehose, included these lines in a letter to Burns before she embarked on the *Roselle* in February 1792, to sail the harrowing five thousand mile, two month journey to Kingston, Jamaica.

QUESTION 45

Name the doctor who attended Burns during his last illness?

Answer

Dr William Maxwell.

Dr Maxwell was the son of James Maxwell of Kirkconnell, was born in 1760 and educated at the Jesuit College at Dinant in France. Whilst on the continent, he became a member of the National Guard, and, it is said, was present at the execution of Louis XVI. He returned in 1794, settled in Dumfries and there met Burns. It was Dr Maxwell who prescribed sea bathing and horse riding as a possible cure for Burns' illness, either of which may have hastened Burns' death.

Before his death, Burns presented Dr Maxwell with his pair of excise pistols, now in the Museum of Scottish Antiquities in Edinburgh. Jean Armour named her son Maxwell after him. He was in attendance at the birth, the day of the poet's funeral.

QUESTION 46

"My partner was a scoundrel of the first water who made money by the mystery of thieving." To whom was Burns referring?

Answer

David Peacock of Irvine.

In the autumn of 1781, at the age of twenty three, Burns went to Irvine to learn flax dressing and remained there until the following spring. As Robert and his brother Gilbert grew flax, Robert thought it was a profitable idea to dress it themselves. But the venture came to an untimely end for, in Burns' own words, "The shop took fire, and burnt to ashes, and I was left like a true poet, not worth a sixpence."

Whilst in Irvine, Burns stayed with a Mr Peacock and his wife, perhaps a distant relative of Burns' mother who, in Burns' opinion was a rogue. Because of bad working conditions, and the lack of good food, Burns took an illness (pleurisy) and had to return to Lochlea Farm.

QUESTION 47

To whom was Burns writing when he wrote "Save me from the horrors of a jail."

Answer

James Burnes, a cousin of the poet.

Burnes was a lawyer in Montrose although there is not much evidence to support any claim that Burns and his cousin were very close to each other. Burns wrote his cousin on the 17th February, 1784 to inform him of his father's death.

"That melancholy event which for some time past we have from day to day expected."

Little news passed between them until 12th July, 1796, when Burns wrote begging him to send £10.

"O' James! Did you know the pride in my heart, you would feel doubly for me! Alas! I am not used to beg! . . . Forgive me for once more mentioning by return of post. Save me from the horrors of jail."

James sent the money and, after Burns' death, a further £5 to Jean Armour, and an offer to take young Robert and rear him as one of his own. Jean declined the kind offer.

QUESTION 48

To whom was Burns referring when he said,

"The worthiest and best-hearted man living and a man of real genius."

Answer

Allan Masterton.

Masterton was appointed joint teacher of writing and music on 26th August, 1795 in the High School, Edinburgh: prior to this he taught writing in Stevenlaw's Close, High Street, Edinburgh, where Burns met him. He was the composer and "hero" of "Willie Brewed", along with the composition "Beware o' Bonnie Ann".

QUESTION 49

Who was "Bonnie Ann"?

Answer

Bonnie Ann was Masterton's daughter who married a Dr Derbyshire who practised at Bath and London.

QUESTION 50

Who was described as "very pleasant and winning, though not a beauty"?

Answer

Mary Campbell, "Highland Mary".

According to Burns' mother, the poet directed his attention to Mary Campbell after being "turned down" by Jean Armour who was at that time – March 1786 – staying in Paisley. Mary Campbell was the daughter of Archibald Campbell of Daling, by Dunoon, born in 1763. The description was given by Mrs Todd, a married daughter of Gavin Hamilton, who employed Mary as a nursemaid in Mauchline. Two of Burns' best known works were dedicated to Mary Campbell, being "Ye Banks and Braes" and "To Mary in Heaven".

QUESTION 51

To whom did Burns dedicate the poem "The Brigs of Ayr"?

Answer

John Ballantine.

Ballantine was a merchant banker in the town of Ayr, and a patron of Burns. Whilst Dean of Guild, he was instrumental in bringing about the building of the new bridge in Ayr in 1791. Burns was thanking Ballantine for having hoisted him "up to the court of Gentiles, in the Temples of Fame."

According to Gilbert Burns, the poet's brother, Ballantine offered to lend Burns the necessary money needed to pay Wilson, the Kilmarnock printer, for a second Kilmarnock edition, this along with advice to try his luck in Edinburgh for a publisher. He took his advice, but not the money.

QUESTION 52

Who were "The Ronalds of the Bennals"?

Answer

William Ronald and his two daughters Jean and Anne. The Bennals was a two hundred acre farm in Tarbolton owned by William Ronald, and Burns' poems "The Ronald's of the Bennals" satirises their wealth, which gave William Ronald the "title" of the Laird.

His daughter, Jean was baptised in October 1759, her sister Anne in June 1767. Gilbert Burns had his "sights" on Jean, the elder of the two, but she married John Reid, a farmer at Langlands. In November 1789, William Ronald went bankrupt, and Burns in a letter, sent to Gilbert informing him of the event, suggested that Ronald may now "feel a little retaliation from those who thought themselves eclipsed by him."

QUESTION 53

"Maxwell, if merit here you crave.

PROCESSION OF ST JAMES' LODGE OF FREEMASONS
THROUGH TARBOLTON
(*See Question 246*)

THE TWA BRIGS OF AYR
See Questions 51, 71, 101, 150

25

That merit I deny:
You save fair Jessie from the grave!
An angel could not die."
Who was "the angel"?

Answer
Jessie Staig.

Jessie was the daughter of David Staig, Provost of Dumfries and was born in 1775. She married Major William Miller, son of the landlord of Ellisland. Burns, writing to Mrs Dunlop in 1794 said of her, "A lovely creature of sixteen, was given over by the physician, who openly said that she had but a few hours to live." She was attended by Dr Maxwell, who also attended Burns during his last illness. She died in 1801, at the relatively young age of 26.

QUESTION 54
Who was Betty Davidson?

Answer
The widow of a cousin of Burns' mother, who frequently stayed with family. Burns said, in an autobiographical letter that she had "The largest collection in the country of tales and songs concerning devils, ghosts, fairies, brownies, witches, warlocks, spunkies, kelpies, elf candles, dead-lights, wraiths, apparitions, contraips, inchanted towers, giants, dragons and other trumpery."

QUESTION 55
Whom did Burns describe as, "D'rymple mild, D'rymple mild"?

Answer
The Rev William Dalrymple in "The Kirk's Alarm."

He was the son of the Sheriff Clerk of Ayr, James Dalrymple, and became junior minister of Ayr parish in 1746 and remained so for ten years. In 1779, St Andrews University conferred the degree of Doctor in Divinity upon him, and in 1781 he became the Moderator of the General Assembly. He owned Mount Charles Estate, which is very close to Burns Cottage at Alloway, and was the uncle of Burns' friend, Robert Aiken. He died in 1807.

QUESTION 56
What were the pen names Burns and Mrs McLehose used when corresponding?

Answer
Clarinda and Sylvander.

26

ELLISLAND
See Questions 57, 63, 69, 216, 299

MOSSGIEL
See Questions 74, 245

27

It is difficult to think of Burns without giving a thought to "Clarinda" and their love affair, which inspired that well known love song "Ae Fond Kiss", but it should be remembered it was not a long affair. From the first to the last meeting was only about four years. "Clarinda's" married name was Agnes McLehose; she was the daughter of a Glasgow surgeon, Andrew Craig. She met Burns at a tea party in the home of a Miss Nimmo on 4th December, 1787 and their last meeting took place in Edinburgh 6th December, 1791. "Clarinda" was born in 1759 and died in 1841.

QUESTION 57
When Burns was at Ellisland, he was given the loan of a horse. From whom did he get it?

Answer
William Nicol.
Nicol was the son of a tailor in Ecclefechan and was born at Dumbretton, Parish of Annan in 1744 and left fatherless at a very early age. He attended Annan Grammar School and at Edinburgh University first studied for the ministry and then medicine and in 1774 became classics master in the High School in Edinburgh. He remained there for twenty one years after which he ran a school of his own until his death, two years later.

QUESTION 58
Who was the subject of the "Epitaph on Wee Johnie"?

Answer
The Rev John Kennedy of Ochiltree and Terrelges.
Most certainly not John Wilson, the printer of the Kilmarnock Edition. On the finding of the original manuscript in 1909, the *Glasgow Herald* judged that Burns knew Kennedy in both Ayrshire and Dumfriesshire.

QUESTION 59
Whence is the reference "Old Q" taken?

Answer
William Douglas, 3rd Earl of March, and 4th Duke of Queensberry. The bachelor Duke earned Burns' disapproval for his deception of George III and for his general abuse of his wealth and position.

QUESTION 60
Who was the "Scottish Milkmaid"?

28

Answer
Janet Little (later Richmond).
A poetess whom, according to Mrs Dunlop, Burns ignored. Mrs Dunlop tried to interest Burns in the edition of Janet Little's poetry published in 1792. It could be that Burns considered a poet to be unfit to become a critic of a fellow-poet, and that silence was the kindest form of criticism. That apart, Burns had recently left Ellisland and settling into the Excise, he probably had enough troubles of his own.

QUESTION 61
Who took the pseudonym "Cato"?

Answer
Captain Robert Riddell when writing an essay on parliamentary reform in the *Edinburgh Gazetteer*. As neighbours, Riddell and Burns were friends. Riddell was liberal in politics and, as "Cato", was persuaded by Burns to write this essay on the need for electoral reform.

QUESTION 62
Who are buried in close proximity in the kirkyard of the Laigh Kirk, Kilmarnock?

Answer
Tam Samson, Dr McKinlay and the Rev John Robertson.
Samson, a local businessman and sportsman, was a close friend of Burns. McKinlay and Robertson were, respectively, the senior and junior ministers in the Laigh Kirk.

QUESTION 63
Who lived at Friars' Carse?

Answer
Robert Riddell.
The property was contiguous with Burns' farm at Ellisland. They became great friends until one evening when, flushed with after dinner drinking and against Burns' advice, they organised a playful and innocent "Sabine Rape" on the lady guest. The joke mis-fired and Burns was made the scapegoat.

QUESTION 64
"Friend of the Poet, tried and leal
Wha, wanting thee, might beg and steal"
Who is this friend of Burns?

29

Answer

John Mitchell, Collector of Excise in Dumfries.

Mitchell testified to Burns' efficiency as an excise officer. It is reported that Burns sent several copies of his manuscripts to Mitchell but that the Mitchell family lost them after his death.

QUESTION 65

When Burns' remains were placed in the mausoleum in St Michael's Kirkyard, Dumfries, who requested to be buried in his original, lowly grave?

Answer

Agnes Eleanor Dunlop Perochon, eldest daughter of Mrs Dunlop of Dunlop. Mrs Perochon was a direct descendant of Sir William Wallace and her gesture shows the affection this family held for Burns. The original grave can still be seen in the south east corner of the churchyard.

QUESTION 66

What proof is there that John Brown was the "Mauchline Wag"?

Answer

Burns' manuscript has a preamble referring to "Johanne's Fuscus" (John Brown) *quondam horolgiorum faber* (one time clock-maker) "In Mauchline". Argument raged as to the identity, but the late discovery of Burns' manuscript containing the "Epitaph on the wag in Mauchline," cleared up any doubts as to the identity.

QUESTION 67

About whom was Burns writing when he described him as "drinking, swearing, and playing cards"?

Answer

Gavin Hamilton.

Hamilton was Burns' lawyer friend who is thus described in "Holy Willie's Prayer". Hamilton, of Mauchline Castle, was not only Burns' friend and landlord but the scourge of hypocritical churchgoers.

QUESTION 68

Who won the "Whistle" competition?

Answer

Alexander Fergusson of Craigdarroch. Fergusson drank two other aristocrat companions "under the table" to win possession of this Danish relic. Burns was a spectator at Robert Riddell's house, Friars' Carse, where the challenge took place.

30

SECTION 2

QUESTION 69

Burns was required to build his own farmhouse at Ellisland. When was the building completed?

Answer

June 1790.

The contract to build the house was given to Thomas Boyd, mason and contractor in Dumfries. The same year Thomas Boyd was given the contract to build the New Bridge over the Nith at Dumfries.

QUESTION 70

Where did Burns meet Lord Daer?

Answer

In the home of Professor Dugald Stewart, Catrine House.

Catrine House is a mile south west of the village of Catrine, in Ayrshire, and was the seat of Professor Dugald Stewart, the philosopher. Catrine is a small town and lies in the Parish of Sorn, on the River Ayr, two and a half miles from Mauchline. Burns dined with Dugald Stewart at Catrine House on 23rd October, 1786, and there met Lord Daer, the son of the Earl of Selkirk.

QUESTION 71

Where was the "Ducat Stream" mentioned in "The Brigs of Ayr"?

Answer

It was a ford, just above the auld brig in Ayr.

Before the old bridge was built, the ford was the only means of entry into the town.

QUESTION 72

The villagers in Alloway in 1891 made a successful protest regarding Alloway Kirk. What was the protest?

Answer

To stay the removal of the bell from Alloway Kirk. The kirk was built in 1516 and was last used for worship in 1756. When the parishes of Ayr and Alloway were joined in 1891 by the Boundary Commissioners, a proposal was made to remove the old bell.

QUESTION 73

At which pier did the boat rock in the song "The Silver Tassie"?

ALLOWAY KIRK, 1805
See Questions 72, 121

FARM OF LOCHLEA, TARBOLTON
See Questions 75, 243

Answer
Leith pier.

With the proceeds of his poems published at Kilmarnock, Burns proposed to seek his fortune in the West Indies. His bags were packed and ready for his departure from the pier at Leith, but, with the prospects of a second edition of his poems, the plan was abandoned. It is said the song was suggested to Burns on witnessing a young military officer parting from his sweetheart on the pier at Leith.

QUESTION 74
When he wrote "To a Mouse" at which farm was Burns staying?

Answer
Mossgiel.

"It is difficult to decide" writes Currie, "whether this address should be considered as serious or comic". The descriptive part is admirable, the moral reflection beautiful.

QUESTION 75
On which Ayrshire farm was Burns living when he took dancing lessons?

Answer
Lochlea.

Lochlea is about two and a half miles north east of Tarbolton, and just over three miles north west of Mauchline. The farm was one hundred and thirty acres, and was owned by David McLure, who leased it to William Burnes at the annual rental of one pound per acre. It was at Lochlea, that Burns found the need for companionship and made many friends, including James Findlay, John Wilson (Death and Dr Hornbook), David Sillar and John Rankine, and not forgetting the growing interest for the "lasses". In the winter of 1779, Burns attended dancing classes to, as he put it, "Give my manners a brush", much against his father's wishes. Early in 1781, along with playing an active part in the Tarbolton Bachelors Club, he had a strong love affair with Alison Begbie, and went to stay in Irvine to learn flax dressing, where he took ill and had to return to Lochlea. In the summer of 1782, came the "last straw" when, a warrant of sequestration was served upon the poet's father. Burnes, though old and near to death, took his case to Court of Session in Edinburgh, and won, at the expense of all his savings.

He died a few days later on 13th February, 1784.

QUESTION 76
In which Ayrshire village was "Kirkton Jean" an innkeeper?

Answer
Kirkoswald.
"Kirkton Jean", real name Jean Kennedy, was born in Crossraguel, and kept a small inn along with her sister. They were known as "The Leddies", though Burns, in his poem "Tam O'Shanter" referred to it as "The Lord's House".

QUESTION 77
Where would you find a portrait of John Wilson, the printer of the Kilmarnock Edition?

Answer
The Dick Institute in Kilmarnock.
Wilson, who was born in the same year as Burns, was the son of a shopkeeper. He started his printing business in 1780. John served as a baillie on Kilmarnock Town Council, but in 1810 he sold his business and moved to Ayr where he died in 1821. His shop was at the corner of King Street and Waterloo Street, the printing office was on the third flat of a tenement in Waterloo Street, Kilmarnock.

QUESTION 78
Where in Kilmarnock would you find the monument and statue to Burns?

Answer
Kay Park.
The erection of a statue in Glasgow by shilling subscriptions gave an impetus to similar schemes throughout Scotland. The memorial building consists of two storeys and a tower, and rises to a height of seventy five feet, the work of a local architect, R S Ingram. The statue of the poet is the work of W G Stevenson, Edinburgh, modelled on Nasmyth's portrait of Burns. The memorial cost two thousand pounds, and was opened by Col. Alexander of Ballochmyle on the 9th August, 1879. The museum, within the monument, is reputed to be the richest in the world in respect of Burns MSS.

QUESTION 79
Where would you find the tombstone to Mary Morrison?

Answer
Mauchline Kirkyard, Ayrshire.
Mary Morrison, the heroine of the lovely song of the same name, was the daughter of Adjutant Morrison of Mauchline who had attained the

34

age of eighty upon his death. She was a girl of only sixteen when she first drew the attention of the poet. The following inscription can be seen on the tombstones, erected in 1825 in Mauchline Kirkyard:

In memory of Adjutant John Morrison of the 104th Regiment, who died at Mauchline 16th April, 1804, and in the 80th year of age, also his daughter – The poet's "lovely Mary Morrison" – who died 29th June, 1791, Age 20: and his second spouse, Ann Tomlinson, who died 6th September 1831, aged 76.

QUESTION 80
In which parish is the inn called the "Whitefoord Arms"?

Answer
Mauchline.

It was situated, but has now been replaced by a later building, on the Cowgate, now Castle Street, opposite the parish church. The Court of Equity, a secret bachelors' club, held their meetings here. The club, of which Burns was "perpetual president", met "To search out, report, and discuss the merits and demerits of the many scandals that crop up from time to time in the village". John Dove or Dow ("Johnnie Doo") was the proprietor of the inn.

QUESTION 81
Burns described the place as venerable, respectable, hospitable, social, convivial, imperial queen of cities. To which city was he referring?

Answer
Auld Reekie – Edinburgh.

Burns sent a letter containing these words on May 5th, 1787, to Mr Fyfe, surgeon, Edinburgh, on the day he left Edinburgh to commence his border tour with Ainslie.

QUESTION 82
Where, in Burns' opinion, was "The only tolerable inn in the place"?

Answer
Baillie Edward Wigham's inn in Sanquhar.

Sanquhar is a town in upper Nithsdale, twenty six miles from Dumfries, and Burns had to pass through it when riding between the Isle and Mauchline. The night he stayed at this inn was a cold winter one, and he was asked to leave and ride twelve miles further on to find an inn at New Cumnock, to allow the innkeeper to accommodate the funeral cortège of Mrs Lucy Oswald of Auchencruive. Burns was very bitter

35

about the treatment he received and penned "Ode Sacred to the Memory of Mrs Oswald of Auchencruive", which plainly expresses his disgust over the incident.

QUESTION 83
Name the five burghs mentioned in the poem "The Five Carlins".

Answer
Annan, Dumfries, Kirkcudbright, Lochmaben and Sanquhar.

Burns wrote this ballad on the occasion of the contest for the Representation in Parliament of the Dumfries Group of Burghs in 1798.

"Whisky Jean" stands for Kirkcudbright.
"Maggie by the banks o' the Nith" – Dumfries.
"Blinking Bess of Annandale" – Annan.
"Black Joan frae Chrichton-Peel" – Sanquhar.
"Marjory o' the mony lochs" – Lochmaben.

QUESTION 84
Where did Burns study mensuration, surveying and dialling?

Answer
Kirkoswald – Ayrshire.

In 1775, Burns' father sent Robert to Kirkoswald to further his education under the village dominie Hugh Rodger. Whilst there, he studied mensuration, surveying and dialling in an effort to further his skill as a farmer. He shared an attic with his friend, John Niven of Maybole in the farmhouse of Ballochniel.

QUESTION 85
Where is the River Doon?

Answer
The Doon flows from Loch Doon, on the borders of Ayrshire and Kirkcudbrightshire, to the Firth of Clyde, which it enters about ten miles West of Ayr. It divides the Ayrshire district of Carrick and Kyle. Burns has made many references to it, notable in "Tam O'Shanter" and the song "Ye Banks and Braes O' Bonnie Doon".

QUESTION 86
Where did Burns go when he went into hiding to escape the wrath of James Armour?

Answer
Old Rome Forest.

36

HOUSE WHERE BURNS DIED IN DUMFRIES
See Question 87

The house occupied by Jean Brown, an aunt of Burns on his mother's side, along with her husband James Allen was close to John Wilson the printer in Kilmarnock.

QUESTION 87
Where is the second house that Burns took in Dumfries, and what was its significance in his story?

Answer
Mill Street (now Burns Street).

Burns moved to this second house in May 1793, and it is now under the care of The Dumfries Burns Club. The poet died there on the 21st July, 1796, leaving his wife, Jean Armour, to reside there until her death in 1834, and the house is now a leading Burns Museum. His first home in Dumfries was in The Wee Vennel, now Bank Street, a second floor flat, comprising three rooms and kitchen. It is not open to the public.

QUESTION 88
In a letter to George Thomson, Burns said, "For these past years it has been my favourite howff." To which building was he referring?

Answer
The Globe Tavern at Dumfries.

It was, and still is, an inn in Dumfries, then owned by Mr and Mrs Hyslop. Anna Park, with whom Burns had a close association, was a niece of Mrs Hyslop.

QUESTION 89
When Burns said in a letter to George Thomson, "This unfortunate, wicked little village", to which village was he referring?

Answer
Ecclefechan.

Ecclefechan is a small village in Dumfriesshire, the birthplace of Thomas Carlyle, and was twice visited by Burns. On the second visit, he wrote to Thomson on 7th February, 1795, "You cannot have any idea of my predicament in which I write you. In the course of my duty as supervisor (in which capacity I have acted of late) I came yesternight to this unfortunate, wicked, little village."

QUESTION 90
Where and what is Adamhill?

Answer

A farm in the parish of Craigie, two miles from Lochlea, then occupied by John Rankine.
"Rough, rude, ready witted Rankine,
The wale o' cocks for fun an' drinking!"
Rankine's daughter Anne, claimed to have been the subject for the song "Corn Rigs".

QUESTION 91

Where would you find Highland Mary's Bible?

Answer

Burns Monument at Alloway.

It is a two volume copy, and on the title page of volume one is a date, 1782, and a price mark of five shillings and six pence. On the fly leaf, in Burns' handwriting, is written the following:
"And ye shall not swear by my name falsely: I am the Lord LEVIT. XIX. 12"
In the second volume, also in Burns' handwriting, is the following:
"Thou shall not forswear thyself but shall perform unto the Lord thine oaths MATH.V.38"

QUESTION 92

Where was Burns baptised?

Answer

In the Auld Kirk, Ayr.

The Auld Kirk is situated between High Street and the river, and, although re-constructed internally, it is in much the same condition as in Burns' day. Burns was baptised by Dr William Dalrymple of "The Kirk's Alarm", and is interred in the churchyard. Burns was a fairly regular attender at the church along with his parents whilst residing in Alloway.

QUESTION 93

Who was Dr Thomas Blacklock, where was he born, when did he die and where is he buried?

Answer

He was the son of a bricklayer, born in Annan, Dumfriesshire in 1721. In the first year of his life he lost his sight as a result of smallpox. He studied Divinity at Edinburgh University, and was ordained minister of Kirkcudbright in 1762, retiring to Edinburgh on a small annuity in 1765. He died in 1791 and is buried in Cuthbert's Chapel of Ease.

BURNS' MONUMENT AND AULD BRIG O'DOON (left), ALLOWAY
See Questions 91, 121, 123, 136

TAM O'SHANTER INN
See Questions 101, 108, 118, 121, 286

40

QUESTION 94
Where is Burns' Cottage?

Answer
Alloway, Ayrshire.

The cottage, with the land surrounding it, was sold by William Burnes in 1781 to the Incorporation of Shoemakers in Ayr, for £160. Shortly before 1800, it was turned into an alehouse and remained so until 1881, when it was acquired by the Alloway Burns Monument Trustees. The original building was conceived and erected by the poet's father, and this is open to the public.

QUESTION 95
Name the theatre in Dumfries that Burns was wont to patronise?

Answer
The Theatre Royal; although much altered, it still exists today.

QUESTION 96
Where was the "Elbow Tavern"?

Answer
Mauchline.

Continuing Castle Street, where Burns set up house, is a narrow street at right angles – an elbow. Here was the tavern which Burns used more as a meeting place than a public house.

QUESTION 97
Where are Tam O'Shanter and Souter Johnnie buried?

Answer
Kirkoswald Kirkyard.

Douglas Graham, "Tam", and John Davidson, "The Souter", are buried at opposite ends of the ruined church.

QUESTION 98
The "Whistle" was the prize for a drinking competition of that name. Where is it now?

Answer
In Caprington Castle, Kilmarnock.

The whistle, of Danish origin, was competed for at Friars' Carse between Sir Robert Lawrie, Robert Riddell, and Alex Fergusson. Out-drinking the other two, Fergusson blew the winning blast on the whistle and took possession of it. John McMurdo was judge, and Burns was a witness at the competition.

41

BURNS' BIRTHPLACE, ALLOWAY, 1805
See Questions 94, 113, 226, 274, 275, 276, 292

INTERIOR OF BURNS' BIRTHPLACE

QUESTION 99
Which inn in Glasgow was most favoured by Burns as a stopping-over place?

Answer
The Black Bull inn on the corner of Virginia and Argyle Street. Demolished in 1958.

QUESTION 100
"If providence has sent me here
'Twas surely in his anger."
Where?
Answer
Inveraray.

Little or nothing remains of Burns' writings on his West Highland tour. He wrote of "savage mountains, savage flocks (supporting) savage inhabitants". Once more he rebelled against the abuses of landowners against their tenants. This brief poetical influence might have been sparked by the ever-touchy Burns imagining himself to be insulted or ignored at an inn in Inveraray.

QUESTION 101
In which year did Ayr become a Royal Burgh?

Answer
In 1202.

Burns called it:
"Auld Ayr, wham ne'er a town surpasses
For honest men and bonnie lassies"
It is a busy, thriving market town and holiday resort, with a strong historical background. It was in Ayr that Wallace struck the first blow for Scottish independence, and in the castle near Turnberry, Bruce began the struggle that ended in Bannockburn. Its many and varied attractions include the Tam O'Shanter Inn in High Street (now a museum); the Toll Booth; a fine statue of Burns in the centre of the town gazing in the direction of his birthplace, Alloway; the Auld Kirk, and the Auld Brig, "The Brigs of Ayr".

QUESTION 102
What took place at Dalswinton Loch?

Answer
The first steamship was launched.

Dalswinton Mansion belonged to Burns' landlord Patrick Miller, and was situated on the side of the river Nith. On its loch the first steamship was launched by Miller on the 14th October, 1788. The designer was William Symington and on board the ship with Miller were, among others, Nasmyth, Harry Brougham and Burns.

SECTION 3

QUESTION 103
"Struggling student as I am, I will not quit the pen on Burns as long as I breathe." By whom was this said?

Answer
Toshio Namba, Professor, Nihon University, who visited Ayr in 1965. His latest works include *Poetry of Robert Burns, Nature and Life.*

QUESTION 104
Who was it said of Burns: "He is great in verse, greater in prose and greatest in conversation"?

Answer
William Robertson, D.D., Principal of Edinburgh University.
    Robertson declared that he had "scarcely ever met with any man whose conversation displayed greater vigour than that of Burns. His poems had surprised, his prose compositions appeared even more wonderful, but the conversation was a marvel beyond all."

QUESTION 105
By whom was this said of Burns: "He had the Scottish gift of making his vices more amiable than other people's virtues"?

Answer
George Bernard Shaw.
    It is on record that an Edinburgh man, Mr William Priest, wrote a letter to George Bernard Shaw on Hogmanay 1933, expressing his amazement at the fact that this great man had never expressed his opinion of the Scots bard. The following reply was dated 17th February, 1934:
    "Burns was an authentic poet whose word-music has always given me the greatest pleasure and, who had the Scottish gift of making his vices more amiable than other people's virtues. He also had a great man's sense of human values, he gave a crushing demonstration of the artistic superiority of living dialect to Academic letters."

Mr Priest died in 1950, and his stepsister, Mrs M Pirie, made the Burns Federation the recipient of the letter, which can be seen in the Burns House Club, Glasgow.

QUESTION 106
What shameful act did David Williamson commit when he discovered that Burns was dying?

Answer
Pressed him to settle a financial account. Williamson was a tailor who had made for Burns a uniform for the Royal Dumfries Volunteers. On hearing of Burns' approaching death, Williamson's lawyer sent Burns the account and a threat of imprisonment for non-payment.

QUESTION 107
In the poem "To a louse", Burns mentions a bonnet, "But Miss's fine Lunardi!" How did the name Lunardi come into being?

Answer
A Lunardi was a balloon shaped bonnet.
It was so named after Vincenzo Lunardi, of Italian extraction who claimed to be "The first aerial traveller in the English atmosphere". In 1784, he made balloon ascents from sites in and around London, also from Edinburgh and Glasgow the following year. He was born in 1759 and died in 1806.

QUESTION 108
Who played an important role in the preservation of the "Tam O'Shanter Inn," thus enabling it to be made into a museum?

Answer
John Gray.
John Gray, a past president of the Burns Federation, earned his livelihood as a master baker when he came to live in the town of Ayr. His business was in George Street, just opposite the "Auld Brig". He was a member of Ayr Town Council in 1956 and made good use of this by utilising his influence to launch a successful appeal for the preservation of the inn for all time. His knowledge of Burns was spread far afield, and he travelled extensively, including Russia. He was a guide, friend and courier to Samuel Marshak when the Russian visited Burns country. Mr Gray carried out the same duty when Toshio Namba, who has translated Burns into Japanese, visited Ayrshire. Mr Gray died on September 27th, 1976 at the age of eighty five years.

QUESTION 109
Apart from Burns, which other poet had works put out by Wilson of Kilmarnock?

Answer
John Lapraik.
Lapraik was born in 1727, at Dalquhram, and was twice married. First to Margaret Rankine, sister of John Rankine of Adamhill, and second to Janet Anderson. He was a farmer-bard, until the failure of the Ayr bank in 1783, when he was compelled to sell off his property, and it is on record that he was imprisoned for debt. Later, he moved to Muirkirk and took lease on a farm, finally settling in Muirshill becoming an innkeeper and postmaster. One of Lapraik's poems appeared in the *Scots Musical Museum* in 1773, "When I upon your bosom lean". Lapraik died in 1807.

QUESTION 110
What's "Aye the cheapest lawyer's fee"?

Answer
"To taste the barrel" from "Scotch drink".
Burns sent a copy of this to his friend Robert Muir, wine merchant, Kilmarnock, on the 20th March, 1785, suggested presumably by Ferguson's "Caller Water".

QUESTION 111
What did Burns describe as "Pycoated Guardians of Escutcheon's"?

Answer
Heraldry.
It is known that Burns had a knowledge of the art of heraldry possibly gained from Captain Grose. This knowledge we find in some of his works, i.e. "A man's a man", "Battle of Sherra Moor" and "Election Ballad".

QUESTION 112
Name the artist responsible for the widely accepted likeness to Burns.

Answer
Alexander Nasmyth.
Nasmyth was the son of an Edinburgh architect (Michael Nasmyth) who sent him to the Edinburgh Academy of Art to study under Alexander Runciman. When seventeen years of age, he studied under Allan Ramsay in London, and later visited Rome to further his studies.

Returning to Edinburgh, he painted portraits of several of the nobility. Creech, Burns' publisher, asked Nasmyth to do a portrait of Burns to illustrate the first Edinburgh Edition, this he did gratis. The engraving of it was carried out by Walker after an unsatisfactory attempt by John Buego, a fellow engraver. Burns received the original by Nasmyth, and his son Colonel William Nicol Burns presented it to the Scottish National Gallery, where it now hangs. Nasmyth was born in 1758 and died in 1845.

QUESTION 113
What was the nature of the startling news to all Burnsians on the 29th July, 1951?

Answer
A fire at the "Auld Clay Biggin", Burns Cottage, Alloway.

The fire was started by a fifteen year old Belfast boy, whilst four hundred visitors were at the cottage at half past three in the afternoon. The flames were confined to about twenty five square yards of the thatched roof above the raftered stable. Fortunately the interior was undamaged. The boy, whose parents were inside the cottage, was playing with lighted matches, but the juvenile court chairman said, "We are satisfied there was no malicious mischief intended," and the boy was discharged.

QUESTION 114
What is a "Wangee Rod"?

Answer
A walking stick.

This stick used by Burns was acquired by the Burns Monument and Cottage Trustees, and can be seen in the Cottage Museum at Alloway. It is a Japanese cane, yellow in colour, three feet long, with a silver top and ferrule at the bottom. When Burns received a letter from Mrs Dunlop intimating a son had been born to Mrs Henri, her widowed daughter, Burns, in his reply included the following, "I seized my gilt-headed wangee-rod, an instrument indispensably necessary, in my left hand, in the moment of inspiration and rapture – and stride – stride – quick and quicker – out skipt I among the broomy banks of the Nith to muse over my joy by retail."

QUESTION 115
On what date was the first meeting of the Mauchline Conversation Society held?

47

Answer
October 30th, 1786.

They met once a month in the house of Charles Paton for the purpose of conversing on a given thesis. The fine for non-attendance was fixed at threepence, which was kept and applied to the purchase of such books as the club thought fit, their first purchase was the *Mirror*. Their topics of conversation covered a wide field and the question of love and marriage were frequently on the agenda.

QUESTION 116
Burns said, "We're worn to crazy years thegither;
  We'll toyte about wi' ane anither"
To whom was he referring?

Answer
His horse, Maggie.

The old mare belonged to Burns, and was the subject of his poem, "The Auld Farmer's New Year Morning Salutation to his Auld Mare, Maggie."

QUESTION 117
Burns described him as "A Gash an' Faithfu' Tyke". To whom was he referring?

Answer
Luath.

He was a favourite dog of Burns immortalized in "The Twa Dogs". It is on record that the poor animal met an untimely end at the hands of ruffians.

QUESTION 118
"A consummation devoutly to be wished". On what occasion was this said?

Answer
The opening of the Tam O'Shanter Museum by William Hazlett, who performed the ceremony.

The building was formerly an inn, whence "Tam" made his immortal ride, and was sold to Ayr Town Council for four thousand pounds. Relics of the Burns period were collected and donated from various parts of the country, and were stored in a local bank until the transformation was completed. The museum was open to the public on the 4th August, 1957.

QUESTION 119
Where would you find "Burns Bed"?

Answer

Derbyshire Royal Infirmary.

On the 7th May, 1932, in Ward No 2, a cheque was handed to the president of the Derbyshire Royal Infirmary for the sum of one thousand seventy pounds, one shilling and nine pence for what is known as the "Robert Burns Bed". This was a gift from the Derby Scottish Association and Burns Club. This is not the only bed of its kind, sometimes called "Robert Burns Cot". There are several in various hospitals and infirmaries in both England and Scotland.

QUESTION 120
What was the date of the inauguration of the monument to Burns in George Square, Glasgow?

Answer

January 25th, 1877.

The pioneers for the monument were Mr James Hedderwick, chairman of the Glasgow Burns Club, which was founded in 1859, and Mr John Brown, a commercial traveller. The subscription began in July and within a year, one thousand six hundred and eighty pounds were raised, and a fixed cost of two thousand was agreed upon. Mr George Edwin Ewing, a local sculptor, was given the commission to build it in bronze. It was unveiled by Lord Houghton.

QUESTION 121
Name the annual festival in connection with Burns which is held in the town of Ayr?

Answer

Tam O'Shanter Ride.

The first year this was held was in 1969, and each year it is growing in popularity. The festival commences in High Street outside what is now the Tam O'Shanter Museum, when the principal actor makes his way on horseback through the town to Alloway and the "haunted Kirk", finally arriving at the famous bridge. On arrival, the well-known part of the poem is enacted, and songs and poems are sung and recited by students and faithful Burnsians.

QUESTION 122
Who was the sculptor of the statues of Tam O'Shanter and Souter Johnnie in the Monument at Alloway?

49

Answer

James Thom.

Tam O'Shanter and Souter Johnnie, the "two drouthy cronies" of Burns great poem, were fashioned in rough grained sandstone in the year 1828 by James Thom, a native of Tarbolton parish. Before the realistic figures were returned to Ayr, they were on exhibition throughout the British Isles.

QUESTION 123

Who was mainly responsible for the preservation of the Auld Brig O'Doon after the new bridge was built?

Answer

The Rev. Hamilton Paul.

In 1813, when the new bridge was built, the Auld Brig O'Doon, which was the only bridge across the Doon, linking Kyle and Carrick, was doomed to destruction. It was then the Rev. Hamilton Paul, a preacher, poet and editor, started his petition to the trustees of the roads in the County of Ayr, and stirred up an enthusiasm which ensured its preservation for all time. The Auld Brig stands as it did in Burns' day, but strengthened.

QUESTION 124

What is the purpose of the Burns Federation?

Answer

The purpose of the federation is fourfold. To strengthen and consolidate by universal affiliation the bond of fellowship existing among the members of Burns Clubs. To purchase and preserve manuscripts and other relics connected with Burns. To repair, renew, or mark with suitable inscriptions, any building, tombstone, etc., interesting from their association with the poet. To encourage and arrange school competitions to encourage and stimulate the teaching of Scottish history and literature. The federation also produce, annually, the *Burns Chronicle*.

QUESTION 125

Many inns and hotels have been named after Burns, name a form of public transport named after him.

Answer

A railway engine.

On the 11th April, 1978, William Ross, MP for Kilmarnock and former Secretary of State for Scotland, had the honour of naming an engine "Robert Burns" at the Glasgow Central Station. I think the choice of William Ross, now Lord Ross, most appropriate, as his father and uncle were both firemen/drivers on the railway, and his grandfather, a guard on the railway. About a year previous, an aircraft, DC-10-30 owned by British Caledonian, was christened "Robert Burns" on 31st March, 1977, at Prestwick Airport. This service was rendered by Colonel Bryce Knox, Lieutenant of Ayr and Arran and chairman of the Burns Monument Trust.

QUESTION 126
What did a direct descendent of Burns think the most appropriate memorial to the poet?

Answer
The National Burns Cottage Homes at Mauchline, the opening ceremony of which was performed by the poet's great-granddaughter, Mrs Violet Burns.

QUESTION 127
A statue of Burns was once removed because the poet did not have a college education. Where is the statue now?

Answer
The Scottish National Portrait Gallery.

The statue was designed by Thomas Hamilton, and the subscription for it was started by John Forbes Mitchell of Bombay, in 1812. Flaxman agreed to furnish a life size marble statue for one thousand four hundred pounds, but afterwards offered to do it either in bronze or marble, gratis. The foundation stone was laid in 1831 and actually had three "homes". First, the Library Hall at Edinburgh University, next the National Gallery in 1861, and finally, the Scottish National Portrait Gallery in Queen Street in 1889, where it can be seen today.

QUESTION 128
Who was the first president of the Burns Club at Irvine?

Answer
Dr McKenzie.

The Irvine Burns Club is one of the oldest clubs, having been established in 1826, its vice-president being Burns' friend, David Sillar. The club possesses some most interesting and valuable Burns' MSS, including the printer's first copy for the first edition published in Kilmarnock in 1786 containing the following poems: "The Cottar's Saturday Night"; "The Twa Dogs"; "The Holy Fair"; "The Author's

51

Earnest Cry and Prayer "; "Address to the Deil " and "Scotch Drink ".
It was originally in the possession of Gavin Hamilton, to whom the poet
dedicated his first volume of poems.

QUESTION 129
In which year was the Burns House Museum officially opened at
Mauchline?

Answer
June 6th, 1969.
The museum was opened by Sir Claud Hogart-Alexander of Mauchline, and in doing so, brought fruition to the efforts of the Burns
Federation, the Glasgow Association of Burns Club, the National Burns
Memorial and Cottage Homes and the Mauchline Burns Club, who
fought endlessly in the belief that it should be preserved for future
generations. The restoration took two and a half years to complete. The
upper part of the house is devoted to exhibitions of Burns relics and the
downstairs part of the building is a folk museum illustrating life in
Mauchline at the time of the poet. It was in this house that Jean and
Robert began their married life.

QUESTION 130
"It kindles wit, it waukens lear". What does?

Answer
Drink from "The Holy Fair. "
This piece was composed in the autumn of 1785, and depicts fairly,
albeit somewhat freely, the celebration of the Holy Communion at
Mauchline on the second Sunday of August of that year. It was more like
a "fair" than a Holy Communion, and Burns was not the first to use the
expression "Holy Fair" in the connection. The poem was met by a
storm of abuse from the pulpits, but amid all the railings that ensued, the
clergy and the people alike did not fail to lay its strictures to heart, and a
general improvement in the conduct of all taking part was soon
manifest.

QUESTION 131
Who said of Burns, "I have never seen such another eye in a human
head, although I have met the most outstanding men in my time"?

Answer
Sir Walter Scott.
Walter Scott, when a lad of fifteen and residing with his parents in
George Square, met Burns in early 1787 at the house of Professor

YOUNG WALTER SCOTT MEETS ROBERT BURNS
See Question 131

BURNS AT THE DUCHESS OF GORDON'S ASSEMBLY, 1787
(*from the pictures by Martin Hardie*)

Ferguson in Sciennes Hill House, in Braid Place. The incident is permanently recorded by that fine painting by Hardie, the artist, which now hangs in the Chambers Institute in Peebles.

QUESTION 132
What was the price paid for a Kilmarnock edition in 1786?

Answer
Three shillings.

In 1898, a copy in the original blue cover, in mint condition as when it left the Kilmarnock printers John Wilson in 1786, was sold for five hundred and ninety pounds. Ten years later, Burns Monument and Cottage Trustees paid one thousand pounds; in 1923, the Carysfort Copy fetched one thousand, six hundred pounds. Two years later, the same buyer gave one thousand and seven hundred and fifty pounds for another copy. The Marquis of Bute's copy sold for eight hundred and eighty eight pounds; in 1957, another was sold for six hundred pounds, but a first edition was auctioned in Glasgow in 1987 for £9900.

QUESTION 133
For what reason, if any, do we accept the painting of Burns by Alexander Nasmyth to be the most genuine likeness to the poet?

Answer
Partly from a statement found on the back of the portrait. This statement was signed by Burns' eldest son Robert, and was dated April 28th, 1834, thirty eight years after Burns' death. "I hereby certify that this is the original portrait of the Poet by Alexander Nasmyth, landscape painter in Edinburgh, and is the only authentic portrait of him in existence, or at least the only portrait of the Poet whose authenticity is indisputable."

QUESTION 134
"Ride the Stang" – how was this punishment carried out?

Answer
The offender was forcibly compelled to sit astride a wooden pole, and was carried shoulder high through the streets.

QUESTION 135
"He died a revered figure who had opened a window on to the outside world for the Russian people". To who does this refer?

Answer
Samuel Marshak.

Marshak, a Russian poet and a man of letters, died near Moscow on the 4th July, 1964, and was without a doubt the man who introduced the genius of Burns to the Russian people. He was elected Honorary President to the Burns Federation in Glasgow in 1960 and his translation of Burns sold over a million copies. Of Jewish parents, the son of a soap factory worker, he moved as a youth to Leningrad where he received immense encouragement from Maxim Gorky. He studied at London University from 1912 to 1914 and visited Scotland on two occasions, and received the Lenin Prize for Literature in 1963, four Stalin Prizes and the Order of Lenin.

QUESTION 136
Sir Alexander Boswell was instrumental in which monument to Burns?

Answer
Burns Monument at Alloway.

It was on the 17th March, 1814, that a meeting was called in the town of Ayr, to commence a subsctiption for the erection of a monument to Burns within his native county. A sum of eight hundred pounds was raised by subscriptions, and the commission for the monument was given to the architect, Thomas Hamilton. The foundation was laid on the 25th January, 1819 and was declared open on the 4th July, 1823.

QUESTION 137
When was the Annual Conference of the Burns Federation held in Ayr and Kilmarnock?

Answer
15th September 1935.

On 17th July, 1885, seventeen Burns enthusiasts met at Kilmarnock and founded the Burns Federation, six years later, forty nine clubs had been affiliated.

SECTION 4

QUESTION 138
The second motto Burns used in his proposed coat-of-arms was "Wood-notes wild". From which poet did he borrow these words?

Answer
John Milton and his poem "L'Allegro". It has also been claimed that the words refer to Jean Armour Burns' clear singing voice. Burns coat-

of-arms was registered at the Court of the Lord Lyon; he died before he could matriculate the arms. Three other Burns family coats-of-arms have since been matriculated.

QUESTION 139
What was the "Pea Straw" edition of Burns' poetry?

Answer
Before Creech's copyright had run out, Robert Smith of Paisley brought out an edition of the poems. He was forbidden to sell the books but, on customers buying a pea straw, he gave a copy of the work free. By 1801 Creech's copyright of the 1787 edition had expired, but not for some twenty new pieces in the 1793 edition. Smith's edition of 1801-2 was therefore in breach in respect of these latter poems, and "interdicted".

QUESTION 140
"For lack o' thee I've lost my lass,
  For lack o' thee I scrimp my glass. . ."
For lack of what?

Answer
Bank-notes.
From the poem "Lines Written on a Bank Note", Burns was contemplating emigration when he wrote this on a Bank of Scotland one pound note.

QUESTION 141
Who wrote the verses beginning: "Sir think not with a mercenary view"?

Answer
Certainly not Burns, although the text implies so. *The Burns Chronicle* of 1895 lists almost fifty such spurious poems used to denigrate Burns. Most of these forgeries illustrate Burns remonstrating with the aristocracy over supposed insults. Burnsians ought to know better than to repeat them.

QUESTION 142
What was wrong with the "Kirk of Lamington"?

Answer
Cold wind, colder kirk, a colder preacher, as written in the poem "The Kirk of Lamington".

QUESTION 143
"The Kirk and State can gae to hell. . .", but where would Burns go?

Answer

"And I'll gae to my Anna". A most favoured song by Burns. "The gowden locks of Anna" refers to Anne Park of Dumfries. Here Burns shows the power and beauty of her to exceed the power and strength of even Church and State.

QUESTION 144
Translate "Facts are chiels that winna ding".

Answer

"Facts are fellows that won't fall down".

The poem, "A Dream" was omitted from the Kilmarnock edition. Burns here produces a loyal birthday ode of a different kind, no mealy-mouthings of a Poet Laureate, but the criticism richly deserving of a monarch who had abused his position and had avoided the responsibilities of his high office.

QUESTION 145
In which poem is "The Big Ha' Bible" mentioned?

Answer

"The Cottar's Saturday Night".

This poem was composed towards the close of the year 1785, it is modelled on Fergusson's "The Farmer's Ingle", and it gives a grave description, with pious approval, of an evening in the life of a Scottish peasant family. The "Cottar" says Gilbert Burns, "is an exact copy of my father, in his manner, his family devotion, and exhortations." The poem is dedicated to his good friend, Robert Aitken. The bible referred to by the poet as "The Big Ha' Bible", once his father's pride, was purchased by the Trustees at Sotheby's on July 21st, 1921 for the sum of four hundred and fifty pounds, and can be seen in the East Room in the Cottage Museum, Alloway.

QUESTION 146
"Auld Lang Syne", the best known song in the world, is often misquoted when sung. Name the faults.

Answer

"For the *sake* of . . ."
"Auld lang *zyne* . . ."
"And there's a hand my trusty *friens* . . ."
Countless gatherings have taken up its strains in an overflow of warm-heartedness, but use words not found in the song. Correctly:
"For auld lang syne . . ."
"And auld lang syne . . ."

57

AULD LANG SYNE
See Question 146

"And there's a hand, my trusty fiere . . ."
I'm sure the bard would be happy to know it was fully understood, albeit misquoted. (Fiere = chum).

QUESTION 147
Who was as "Deaf as Ailsa Craig"?

Answer
Meg, in the song "Duncan Gray". This masterpiece of his poet-craft, Burns sent to Thomson in 1792. It became popular almost immediately. Meg wanted no part of "Duncan's wooing" and "turned a deaf ear" to his advances; hence the line "Meg was deaf as Ailsa Craig." Ailsa Craig is a rocky, conical shaped island in the Firth of Clyde, ten miles west by north of Girvan. Two miles in circumference, eleven hundred and twenty nine feet high. There is a lighthouse and it is a favourite haunt for seabirds.

QUESTION 148
"Some books are lies frae end to end,
And some great lies were never penn'd"
These lines open which poem?

Answer
"Death and Dr Hornbook".
One of Burns most amusing poems which, although composed in 1785, was not included in the Kilmarnock edition. To add to his income as a schoolmaster in Tarbolton, John Wilson dabbled in simple medicine. Death claimed he was thus cheated of some of his intended victims. The Devil, here in the guise of death, is made a figure of fun which did not please the church of Burns' day.

QUESTION 149
What was Burns most uncomplimentary poem to womanhood?

Answer
"Willie Wastle".
Argument rages as to where Linkumdoddie, Wastle's home, stood. Some critics find this poem amusing but only misogynists or male audiences could find it so.

QUESTION 150
From which poem came the following lines – "I'll be a brig when ye're a shapeless cairn"?

"The Brigs of Ayr"
It was in the autumn of 1786 that work began on the building of the New Bridge. The old bridge was built in 1232 and by 1786 was found to be in a dangerous condition. While work was in progress, under the direction of Alex Stevens (mason) and John Ballantine (Dean of Guild), Burns wrote "The Brigs of Ayr", a dialogue between the two bridges. In the dialogue, the Auld Brig prophesies to the New, "I'll be a brig when you're a shapeless cairn". In 1877, the New bridge collapsed, the arch at the far end damaged by floods. In 1910, the Auld Brig was extensively restored.

QUESTION 151
What, according to Burns, is "The poor man's dearest friend"?

Answer
Death, from the poem "Man was made to Mourn".
Several of the poems, says Gilbert Burns, "were produced for the purpose of bringing forward some favourite sentiment of the author's. He used to remark to me that he could not well conceive a more mortifying picture of human life than a man seeking work". In casting about in his mind how this sentiment might be brought forward, the elegy "Man was made to mourn" was composed.

QUESTION 152
For which of Burns' song did Felix Mendelssohn compose the music?

Answer
"O, wert thou in the cauld blast"
Several German composers have set Burns' poetry to music. There is little doubt that Mendelssohn was attracted not only to the beauty and love in his poem, but to its tragic composition, shortly before Burns' death.

QUESTION 153
Who spoke these parting words?
And now, my bairns, wi' my last breath, I lea'e my blessing wi' you baith: And when you think upo' your mither, Mind to be kind to ane anither.

Answer
Mailie, Burns' pet ewe, to her lambs.
This poem, "The Death and Dying Words of Poor Mailie" appeared in the Kilmarnock edition. The quotation used shows Burns' love of animals and nature where he often saw order and compassion in a

greater degree than between man and his neighbour.

QUESTION 154
What did the "fause luver" leave?

Answer

The thorn, from "Ye Banks and Braes o' Bonnie Doon".

This song composition ranks among the better known and loved works of Burns. According to report, it is a real life incident of an unhappy love affair, the unfortunate lady was Miss Kennedy. She was the daughter of a gentleman in Carrick, and was deserted by her lover, Captain Montgonery, the son of a wealthy Wigtownshire proprietor.

QUESTION 155
"But while we sing God save the King", who shall not be forgotten?

Answer

"We'll ne'er forget the People" from the patriotic poem "Does haughty Gaul invasion threat?"

Like Wordsworth, Burns welcomed the ideals of the French Revolution, but when it abused its power into greater tyranny than the recent monarchy, he bitterly criticised it. Burns became an important member of the Royal Dumfries Volunteers and the above poem was typical of his condemnation of the new French regime.

QUESTION 156
Name the three references to time of day that Burns makes to the following meeting on the lea-rig?

"I'll meet thee on the lea-rig,
My ain kind dearie O"
    From the poem, "The Lea-Rig".

Answer

(a) The eastern star = sunset.
(b) Bughtin'-time = end of day's work.
(c) When owsen return = oxen returning to byre.

QUESTION 157
What did Burns wish for when he wrote to John Lapraik "That's a' the learning I desire"?

Answer

"Ae spark o' nature's fire," from "Epistle to John Lapraik".

Lapraik was nearly sixty years of age when Burns sought his acquaintance, and died in 1807. He inherited a small croft near Muirkirk, and was a fellow poet.

61

QUESTION 158

The maggots could wind through the inspired leaves but what had they to spare?

Answer

"His Lordship's golden bindings."

This epigram is typical of Burns satire and his dislike of hypocrisy. Aimed at no-one in particular, it highlights an example of insincerity.

QUESTION 159

"Curs'd be the man, the poorest wretch in life". About whom is Burns talking?

Answer

The hen-pecked husband" for whom Burns had no respect and whom he advised to take his wife by "the magic of a switch" and by "kissing her maids".

QUESTION 160

Supply the missing word.

"There's beauty and fortune to get wi' Miss Morton;
But . . . the jewel for me o' them a'."

Answer

"Armour's," from "The Belles of Mauchline".

This short poem tells of six young ladies of Burns' acquaintance in Mauchline, and their attributes. One was fine, one divine, one had wit, another was braw, and one had beauty and fortune. Jean Armour was Burns' choice of them all.

QUESTION 161

"The best laid schemes o' mice an' men . . ." Go where?

Answer

"Gang aft a-gley."

"An' lea'e us nought but grief an' pain for promis'd joy."

From "To a Mouse", on turning her up in her nest with the plough. November 1785.

QUESTION 162

"Their tricks an' craft hae put me daft,
They've ta'en me in, and a' that . . ."

Complete the next two lines.

Answer

"But clear your decks, an' here's the Sex!

I like the jads for a' that."
    From "The Jolly Beggars"
These lines are the last verse of the sailor's song in "The Jolly Beggars", one of Burns' early works of which he hadn't kept a copy. Probably written in November 1785 and now a magnificent piece of theatre.

QUESTION 163
"'Twas then a blast o' Janwar' win' . . ."
Name the poem containing this line.

Answer
"Rantin' rovin' Robin".

In the year 1759, on January 25th, Robert Burns was born in the "Clay Biggin" at Alloway, Ayrshire. A tradition tells of how the cottage gave way to a violent storm soon after the birth of Burns, and how mother and child had to be carried at midnight to the shelter of a neighbour's dwelling, herein, the "Hansel" referred to in the song "Rovin' Robin'".

QUESTION 164
Who wrote "Ca' the Yowes"?

Answer
Whilst Burns rescued it from obscurity and added some stanzas to it, it is popularly ascribed to Tibbie Pagan, an illicit whisky dealer born in New Cumnock. Burns submitted his amended version to Johnson's *Scots Musical Museum* in 1790, and Thomson's *Selected Scottish Airs* in 1794.

QUESTION 165
Fill in the missing word.
    "The . . . ay's the part ay
    That makes us right or wrang"

Answer
The "heart" from "The Epistle to Davie".

This epistle Burns wrote to a brother poet, David Sillar, the son of a small farmer near Tarbolton. It was while Burns was at Ellisland that he was instrumental in procuring subscribers for Sillar's poems, which appeared in a volume printed in 1787. The two lines above appear in the fifth stanza:
    "Nae treasures nor pleasures
    Could make us happy lang;
    The heart ay's the part ay
    That makes us right or wrang."

QUESTION 166
Why did Beelzebub condemn the Highland Society?

Answer
Because it sought to stop five hundred Highlanders emigrating to Canada.

The "Address of Beelzebub", in 1786 to the Rt. Hon. The Earl of Breadalbane, President (of the London based) Highland Society, sees Burns rebel against Highlanders being the property of their landowners. Beelzebub, is proud of Breadalbane and the Highland Society and promised to make the Earl his "right-hand man".

QUESTION 167
What "Makes countless thousands mourn"?

Answer
"Man's inhumanity to man"
From "Man was made to mourn".

"I had an old grand-uncle" writes the poet in a letter to Mrs Dunlop, "with whom my mother lived while in her girlish years: the good old man was long blind before he died, during which time his highest enjoyment was to sit down and cry, while my mother would sing the simple old song of the 'Life and Age of Man'." The end of that first verse reads thus:

"On January the sixteenth day,
As I did lie alone,
With many a sigh and sob did say,
Ah! Man is made to Moan!"

QUESTION 168
According to Burns in what circumstances is it human to step aside?

Answer
When your brother man or sister woman "Gang a kennin wrang" from "Address to the Unco Guid".

This address was an attack on puritan hypocrisy, and we find that in March 1784 Burns wrote in the First Common Place Book, "I have often observed in the course of my experience of human life, that every man, even the worst, have something good about them".

QUESTION 169
"When death's dark stream I ferry o'er
In Heaven itself I'll ask no more
Than . . ."
What?

64

Answer

"Just a Highland welcome".

From the impromptu verse on receiving hospitality (reputedly at Dalnacardoch near Blair Athole) in 1787.

QUESTION 170

Name the two ministers in "The Twa Herds".

Answer

Rev. John Russell, and Rev. Alexander Moodie.

Written probably in 1784, this has been printed at various times since 1799 under the headings of "The Twa Herds", "The Holy Tulyie" and "Unco Mournfu' Tale". The "Herds" were, the Rev John Russell, assistant minister of Kilmarnock, and afterwards, Minister of Stirling; the Rev. Alexander Moodie, parish minister of Riccarton; the two zealous "Auld Light" preachers and, as such, members of the clerical party to whom Burns was opposed on all occasions.

In justice to the poet, it must be mentioned that the piece was not allowed to appear in any edition of his poems printed during his lifetime.

QUESTION 171

What noted work of Burns stems from "Poosie Nansie's", the inn at Mauchline?

Answer

"The Jolly Beggars", written in 1785, and printed in 1799. "Poosie Nansie", the name still in use to the present day, is an inn in the Parish of Mauchline, Ayrshire and was kept by George Gibson, his wife and their daughter. There is no evidence that Burns contemplated ever giving it to the world, on the contrary, he laid it aside, forgotten, until reminded of it by George Thomson in 1793.

QUESTION 172

Who is the "king o' men for a' that"?

Answer

"The honest man" from "A man's a man for a' that".

When Burns sent this poem to Thomson in January 1795, he included the following note, "I do not give you the foregoing song for your book, but merely by way of *vive la bagatelle*; for the piece is not really poetry." He continues, "A great critic on songs says that Love and Wine are exclusive themes for song-writing. The following is on neither subject, and consequently is no song".

QUESTION 173

What is the meaning of "tine" in the song "The Bonnie Wee Thing"?

Answer

Lose.

"I wad wear thee in my bosom,
Lest my jewel I should tine."

QUESTION 174

"For never but by British hands
Maun . . . wrangs be righted"
Whose wrongs?

Answer

British, from "Does haughty Gaul invasion threat?"

This rousing patriotic ballad sometimes titled, "The Dumfries Volunteers", appeared in The *Dumfries Journal*, on the 5th May, 1795. The effect it had on the rustic population outshone all the speeches of Pitt and Dundas, and the sentiments expressed are most appropriate in today's world.

QUESTION 175

"Oh, were I on Parnassus' Hill . . ."
Why?

Answer

"To sing how dear I love thee".

Burns in this poem seeks classical inspiration to express his love, but settles for the more homely River Nith and hills to meet his needs. This muse might be of local origin but his message timeless.

QUESTION 176

Name the "rich" dog in "The Twa Dogs".

Answer

Caesar

The name of the two dogs in the poem "The Twa Dogs", are Caesar and Luath. Caesar was merely a creature of the poet's imagination, created for the purpose of having a chat with Luath. It was at the Penny Dance in Mauchline, within Jean Armour's hearing, that Burns is supposed to have said,

"He wished he could get any of the lasses to like him as well as his dog did."

66

QUESTION 177
Burns wrote of "Bonnie Lesley". Who was she?

Answer

Miss Lesley Baillie of Playfield, Ayrshire. On their way to England the Baillie family visited Burns in Dumfries in 1792 and Burns was so taken by Miss Lesley's beauty that, not only did he write his tribute, but forbade the publisher Thomson from altering the music which Burns had chosen to accompany it.

QUESTION 178
"O wad some Pow'r the giftie gie us
To see oursels . . ."
Complete the line.

Answer

". . . as ithers see us!"

It has been asserted that the "Lady"upon whose bonnet was displayed the "crowlin' ferlie" was one of the "Belles of Mauchline". The moral embraced in the last stanza has made the lines classic.

QUESTION 179
"It is na, Jean, thy bonnie face
Nor shape that I admire . . ."
What did Burns find dearer?

Answer

"But dear as is thy form to me, still dearer is thy mind".

Written in 1788 and one of Burns' many expressions of love to his wife. Jean was a wife in a million and Burns well appreciated this.

QUESTION 180
"Old nature's prentice hand she tried on man". Then what?

Answer

"An' then she made the lasses, O"

From "Green grow the Rashes, O"

The last stanza is perhaps the finest compliment ever paid to "The Lasses" in song, and does without doubt, embrace all of Burns' sentiment for the opposite sex.

QUESTION 181
"Wha first shall rise to gang awa' . . ." is what?

Answer

"A cuckold, coward loun", from "Willie Brew'd a Peck o' Maut".

QUESTION 182

"Need the warld ken . . .". Ken what?

Answer

"Gin a body kiss a body" from "Comin' Thro' the Rye".

QUESTION 183

"O ye wha are sae guid yoursel',
Sae pious and sae holy . . ."
Give the following lines.

Answer

". . . Ye've nought to do but mark and tell your neebour's fauts and folly", from the "Address to the Unco Guid."

This is pre-eminently, as Scott Douglas remarks, "One of those poems whose lines become 'mottoes of the heart'." The last two stanzas, at least, have been generally esteemed as beyond praise.

Then gently scan your brother man,
Still gentler sister woman;
Tho' they may gang a kennin wrang,
To step aside is human:
One point must still be greatly dark,
The moving *Why* they do it:
And just as lamely can ye mark,
How far perhaps they rue it.

Who made the heart, 'tis He alone
Decidedly can try us;
He knows each chord, its various tone,
Each spring, its various bias;
Then at the balance let's be mute,
We never can adjust it;
What's done we partly may compute
But know not what's resisted.

QUESTION 184

Who were "Assembled by Willie"?

Answer

"Ye sons of old Killie" from the poem of that name. Burns was an honorary member of the Kilmarnock Kilwinning Lodge of Freemasons and addressed this compliment to their Worshipful Master, his friend, William Parker

68

QUESTION 185
"My curse upon your venom'd stang
That shoots my tortur'd gums alang,
An' thro' my lug gies mony a twang
Wi' gnawing vengeance."
What in Burns' opinion is the "Hell o' a' diseases"?

Answer
Toothache, from the "Address to the Toothache".

QUESTION 186
Who started the myth that Burns had composed "Tam O'Shanter" in one day?

Answer
John Gibson Lockhart, son-in-law of Sir Walter Scott, aided by the unreliable Allan Cunningham.

Lockhart's biography of Burns in 1828 was full of inaccuracies and Cunningham, one of the sources, was a most unreliable critic. A teenager when Burns died, he invented what he didn't know, and Lockhart among others used his fictions.

QUESTION 187
"An' forward, tho' I canna see . . ."
What did Burns expect the future to hold for him?

Answer
Very little, he could only "Guess and fear".

These lines are contained in the last stanza of his poem "To a Mouse", and sums up his feelings of the past and his future prospects as a farmer as Mossgiel.

"But och! I backward cast my e'e on prospects drear,
An' forward, tho' I canna see, I guess an' fear."

QUESTION 188
Burns composed a ballad closing each line with the letter "O". Name the ballad.

Answer
"My Father was a Farmer".

Of this composition Burns described it as "a wild rhapsody, miserably deficient in versification; but as the sentiments are the genuine feelings of my heart, for that reason I have a particular pleasure in conning it over."

69

QUESTION 189

Who, referring to the poem "Tam O'Shanter", said:
" A vein of gold had been struck and with fruitless regret one reflects on the value of the treasures which Burns might have dug it from."

Answer

Professor Hans Hecht.

Hetch was a German biographer who not only admired Burns, but also fell in love with the Ayrshire landscape having seen it at first hand. In his biography, he claims it was the parish of Mauchline that decided Burns' destiny, adding "These joyous and exuberant years." Professor Hecht was forced to resign his position in Germany because he was anti-Nazi. In 1919 he published his *Robert Burns*, and this was translated in 1936. Unfortunately, he was killed in Berlin during a British air raid.

QUESTION 190

Whose look was "like the morning's eye"?

Answer

"The lass o' Ballochmyle". These most popular lines were addressed and sent to Miss Wilhelmina Alexander of Ballochmyle. Burns sought her permission to publish the song but Miss Alexander did not acknowledge the letter. She never married and in later years was said to have treasured both the letter and the song.

QUESTION 191

To whom was Burns referring when he used the words " Young Royal Tarry Breeks" in the poem "A Dream"?

Answer

Prince William, son of George III, and later William IV. Whilst Burns believed in democracy and in the monarchy, he was quick to criticise any abuses of the systems.

QUESTION 192

One of Burns' most loved songs was described by Sir Walter Scott as "The essence of a thousand love tales". What is the song?

Answer

" Ae Fond Kiss".

This moving love song Burns sent to "Clarinda", Miss Agnes McLehose, from Dumfries on the 27th December, 1791. At about this time "Clarinda" was preparing to set sail for Kingston in Jamaica to "patch up" her marriage, this she never did.

70

QUESTION 193

Name the smith referred to in "Tam O'Shanter".

Answer

John Niven.

John Niven was a blacksmith at Damhouse at Ardlochan in the parish of Kirkoswald, the father of Robert Niven, and had a family of eight children. He introduced wheelcarts into Carrick, replacing the old-fashioned sledges.

"That ev'ry naig was ca'd a shoe on,
The smith and thee gat roarin' fou' on."

QUESTION 194

Who wrote the earlier models for "The Holy Fair" and "The Cottar's Saturday Night"?

Answer

Robert Fergusson, Edinburgh poet, whose influence in the above is seen in the poem "The Farmer's Ingle". He died in a madhouse and, with the first money he ever had, Burns got permission from the Edinburgh magistrates to mark Fergusson's grave with a fine stone which still stands today.

QUESTION 195

What goes with freedom?

Answer

Whisky, from "The Author's Earnest Cry and Prayer".

The excise laws were strictly enforced and Scottish distillers were in a state of alarm. The Scottish nations were roused by the government law and Burns here adds his protest.

QUESTION 196

What was known as the "Stinking" edition of the poems of Burns?

Answer

Part of the 1787 Edinburgh edition where, in the "Address to the Haggis" stinking is used instead of skinking. Due to the huge demand for the publications, the text was re-set during the printing and the two impressions printed simultaneously. This later setting of the type could not have been checked by Burns.

QUESTION 197

The following is the refrain to which song?

71

"Igo, and ago.
Iram, coram, dago?"

Answer
"Ken ye ought o' Captain Grose?"
Grose was an English antiquarian who became a friend of Burns.
They were, indeed, of the same feather — learned, amusing and companionable. Grose it was who spoke Burns into composing "Tam O'Shanter" for publication.

QUESTION 198
"The bridegroom may forget the bride . . .
The monarch may forget the crown . . .
The mother may forget the child . . ."
Give the final lines.

Answer
"But I'll remember thee, Glencairn,
And a' that thou hast done for me!"
In his "Lament for James, Earl of Glencairn", Burns states his respect and warmth for an aristocrat, who had befriended him during his sojourn in Edinburgh. So deeply was Burns moved by the Earl's death, that this tribute was not the result of instant creation but only composed after considerable thought and reflection.

QUESTION 199
Why did Burns exclude "Mary Morrison" from the Kilmarnock edition?

Answer
He didn't think that the Scottish people were ready for such tenderness in poetry. Burns also excluded from this first edition of his poetry such works as "The Jolly Beggars", "Holy Willie's Prayer", "Death and Dr Hornbook", and the "Address to the Unco Guid". Burns knew that the Church and the Establishment would react violently so, as with his songs already composed, he excluded them from the Kilmarnock edition.

QUESTION 200
What amusing song is popularly thought to have been composed during the "Rosamund" incident?

Answer
"The De'il's awa' wi' th' Exciseman".
Tradition has it that the "Rosamund", a smuggling vessel, was

apprehended in the Solway on 27th February, 1792. Burns was one of the principal officers present when reinforcements were ordered. The officer despatched took so long on his errand that Burns controlled his impatience by composing this most popular song.

QUESTION 201
"The Jolly Beggars", a cantata by Burns, is incomplete. Why?

Answer
The manuscript of this excellent piece of theatre was lost by Burns and he forgot its contents.

QUESTION 202
"Swith! to the Laigh Kirk, ane an' a'
An' there tak up your stations . . ."
Then what?

Answer
"Then aff to Begbie's in a raw,
An' pour divine libations"
    From "The Ordination"
The above lines refer to Begbie's Inn where, after divine service, worshippers could slake their thirst. The words "in a raw" referred to the narrowness of the town or bridge where only a single row of pedestrians could pass if any wheeled traffic was using the way.

QUESTION 203
Who was the "Right Reverend Osnaburg" in the poem, "A Dream"?

Answer
Frederick, Duke of York, who was given the bishopric and living of Osnaburg (£20,000 per year) at the age of seven months by his father, George III.

QUESTION 204
What is unusual about Burns' "Epitaph for Tam Samson"?

Answer
The subject of the epitaph did not die, hence Burns' writing the postscript, "Per Contra".
    Samson was a keen hunter and, caught in a prolonged storm, he took shelter – confounding his mourning friends when he eventually returned to Kilmarnock.

73

QUESTION 205

Which poem did Burns refer to when he wrote "A finishing polish that I despair of ever excelling"?

Answer

"Tam O'Shanter". So wrote Burns to Mrs Dunlop of Dunlop at the same time disposing of the fiction that he wrote the poem in a single day.

QUESTION 206

What were the rights of woman in the Burns' poem of that name?

Answer

Protection, Decorum, Admiration as contained in the "Address spoken by Miss Fontenelle" on her Benefit Night in the Theatre Royal, Dumfries, on 26th November, 1792.

QUESTION 207

What, according to festive Burns, didn't Scotland want?

Answer

"Auld Scotland wants nae skinking ware," from "Address to a Haggis".
"Auld Scotland wants nae skinking ware
That jaups in luggies;
But, if ye wish her gratefu' prayer,
Gie her a Haggis!"

QUESTION 208

What was "The Disputed Ode"?

Answer

The "Ode for General Washington's Birthday".
The poetry here is not worthy of Burns and some claim it to be by another hand. "The Tree of Liberty", another American-inspired example of bad poetry is also disputed, but Burns' manuscript survives.

QUESTION 209

How did a Lord Lyon King of Arms describe the state of heraldic knowledge when Burns designed his arms?

Answer

"The art of heraldry was at its lowest ebb". The original design of arms, as was registered at the Lyon Court, contained a shepherd's crook crossed on a rustic flute or whistle; a holly bush represented Culzean

74

"The place of the Holly", as showing Carrick as his birthday. No less than three other coats-of-arms have been matriculated by members of the Burns or Burnes family, and recently Dumfries Burns Howff Club paid almost £800 to have the arms he designed himself, but never registered, approved by the Lord Lyon in Edinburgh.

QUESTION 210
Because of the position he held in the Royal Dumfries Volunteers, Burns was given a full military funeral. What other reasons have been suggested for the large size of the military escort?

Answer
It was feared that the death of so popular a man might start off riots because of the high price of meal.
  The Royal Dumfries Volunteers were the escort and firing party. Some of the other regular Army unit were obviously called in both to line the streets and to be on hand should any trouble arise, as feared by the various authorities.

QUESTION 211
When was Burns' bust placed in Westminster Abbey and what was the important outcome of the service of dedication?

Answer
In 1885.
  This was followed by the formation of the Burns Federation in Kilmarnock as a result of members of that club attending the church service of dedication.

QUESTION 212
The attempt to have Burns appointed as the first Professor of Agriculture at the University of Edinburgh was promoted by whom?

Answer
Mrs Dunlop of Dunlop, who held a very high opinion of Burns' ability. She had plans to have him proposed and elected to the Chair of Agriculture. In his letters to her, dated 21st April and 7th July 1789, Burns thanked her for her offers but himself judged his appointment to the Chair as a non-starter. The post was filled by a nominee of the benefactor.

QUESTION 213
Burns' Christian name is offered in a variety of forms – Rab, Rabbie, Robbie, Robin and even Bobbie. What form did Burns prefer?

75

Answer

Unparalleled licence had been taken with Burns' christian name. Writing to the editor of the *London Star* he asked to be allowed "to correct the address you give me . . . I am simple Mr Robert Burns, at your service".

QUESTION 214

How long had Burns to wait until Creech made his final payment for the first Edinburgh edition?

Answer

From 21st April, 1787 until 27th February, 1789.

Creech was indeed a mean person. Apart from the delay in paying these and other dues, he allowed Burns only a few gratuitous copies of the second Edinburgh edition in 1793 and tried even then to cheat Burns.

SECTION 5

QUESTION 215

What age was Burns when he is reported to have written the first draft of "Tam O'Shanter"?

Answer

John Niven, his room mate at Kirkoswald claimed that he wrote it between his 16th and 17th birthday.

QUESTION 216

Writing from Ellisland Burns said: "(I am) far from every object I love or by whom I am belov'd except. . . ." Fill in the blank.

Answer

Jenny Geddes, his old mare, from a letter to Mrs Dunlop dated 13th June, 1788.

QUESTION 217

When Burns eventually received some money from Creech for the Edinburgh edition, in 1788, what did he do with part of it?

Answer

He sent it to his brother Gilbert towards the upkeep of the family farm.

The Dick Institute, Kilmarnock, owns Gilbert's account book of the loan – £200 at compound interest, less a small grant to the poet's

76

mother and sisters on an annual basis, and the cost of keeping and educating Burns' illegitimate daughter, Elizabeth. In 1820, with money received for his contributions to a new edition of the poet's works he cleared off the debt. Surely a noble gesture for he himself was never far from poverty.

QUESTION 218
How old was Burns when he died?

Answer
Thirty seven.

QUESTION 219
Who insisted upon bestowing a knighthood on Burns?

Answer
Mrs Catherine Bruce, Lady Clackmannan, whose family claimed to be directly descended from Robert the Bruce. At the ceremony she claimed she had more right to confer the honour than had the Hanoverian kings. To please her in her old age, Burns submitted to the ceremony.

QUESTION 220
What is the most recent medical explanation for Burns' death?

Answer
Acute myocarditis in conjunction with auricular fibrillation.

In 1926 Sir James Crichton-Browne concluded that as a result of Burns contracting rheumatic fever as a hard working farm boy, he died of heart disease – endocarditis. This latest cause of death, based on modern medical research, is offered by Dr R. S. Gilchrist of Edinburgh.

QUESTION 221
List the schools or courses of study which went towards Burns' education.

Answer
Formal education under John Murdoch; writing school at Dalrymple; mathematics and mensuration under Rodger in Kirkoswald; French classes and dancing class in Ayr; singing school at Lochlea and Mauchline; Murdoch as tutor 1765-7; Dalrymple, 1772; Kirkoswald, 1775; singing lessons 1777-8; dancing school 1779.

QUESTION 222
What was the "Ça ira" incident?

Answer

The singing of that French Revolutionary song during a performance at the Theatre Royal, Dumfries. Burns was present but did not participate in the singing. Burns wrote to Robert Graham of Fintry on 5th January, 1793, telling of the incident probably to clear himself, as an excise officer, from any suspicion as to his public activities.

QUESTION 223
What was the "Cinder Libel"?

Answer

The critic Henley wrote that Syme had said Burns was "burnt to a cinder" in his Dumfries days. This charge is completely unfounded and without trace or proof. W. E. Henley was an able enough editor and literary critic, he was also one who accepted the fictions of Burns' declining morality in Dumfries. This is one of them.

QUESTION 224
What shameful act did William Creech, the publisher of the first Edinburgh edition of Burns' poetry, commit after Burns' death?

Answer

Although he had purchased the copyright of Burns' then works for only one hundred guineas he refused to give up the copyright for the benefit of Burns' widow and children.

QUESTION 225
Name the person who first challenged Currie's accusation that Burns was a drunkard.

Answer

The Rev James Gray.

Dr James Currie served Burns' family well from the income derived from his biography of the poet. From malice, ignorance or whatever he succeeded in wrongfully destroying Burns' character. As in modern reporting, sensation sells. Gilbert Burns, brother of the poet, said that Currie was wrong but, in order to raise money for the family, he was not to be corrected. Eventually Gray and others spoke out in favour of the poet's character. Modern research supports Gray and condemns Currie.

QUESTION 226
What was the name given by William Burnes to the cottage he built and in which Burns was born?

78

Answer

New Gardens, which was built in the summer and autumn of 1757. The Burns family lived there until the move to Mount Oliphant in 1766.

QUESTION 227

What was the occupation of Burns' brother William?

Answer

A saddler.

The poet more or less adopted William, his youngest brother, as a teenager. He seems to have been, however, an easy-going lad and Burns had him apprenticed as a saddler. He eventually worked at the trade in London where he died of a fever at the age of twenty-three. He greatly respected the poet, who acted as his mentor and paid the medical bills and burial on William's death, a payment Burns could scarcely afford.

QUESTION 228

Of what elite equestrian group was Burns made an honorary member?

Answer

The Caledonian Hunt, who subscribed for one hundred copies of his first Edinburgh edition.

The hunt comprised nobility and country squires interested in the pursuit of field sports. It was an exclusive body, and Burns' election as a member on 10th October, 1792, shows his high standing and destroys the myth of the so-called character decline in Dumfries.

QUESTION 229

Who was Burns' commanding officer in the Royal Dumfries Volunteers?

Answer

Colonel Arent de Peyster.

A British officer of French Protestant origins, de Peyster admired Burns who served as a member of the Volunteers' influential committee which virtually administered the unit.

QUESTION 230

Who was Burns' first biographer?

Answer

Robert Heron, 1764-1807, wrote the first biography of the poet in 1797. Although shrewd in some of his opinions, Heron, like Currie, wrongly wrote of Burns' drinking habits, perhaps, like Henry McKenzie, being jealous of the adulation paid to the ploughman poet.

QUESTION 231
How much money did Burns receive from the publication of the second Edinburgh edition of his poetry, published in 1793?

Answer
None.
He did receive a few complimentary copies but Creech even tried to cheat him with these. Burns had sold the copyright of his works to Creech who, in his greed and business acumen, gave the poet no favours.

QUESTION 232
How many copies were printed for the first Kilmarnock edition in 1786?

Answer
Six hundred and twelve.
The collection of poems sold at 3/- per copy and the whole edition was very quickly sold. So great was the demand for the second (Edinburgh) edition that part way through its printing more type had to be set up to run off a further impression even as that edition was itself being printed.

QUESTION 233
Which newspaper wished to employ Burns as a journalist?

Answer
London Star, and the *Morning Chronicle*.
Burns was in frequent contact with Scottish and English newspapers. Several editors offered him regular journalistic employment. In declining employment Burns wrote: ". . . but in my present (political) situation, I find I dare not accept. . . . My prospect in the Excise is something". May 1794.

QUESTION 234
Did Burns read written or printed music, and could he write down music?

Answer
"Burns could read music, either written or printed, I have seen him write sacred music, but never any other".
This was said by Isabella Burns Begg in 1847, when interviewed by Capt Charles Gray, R.M. on behalf of George F. Graham, who published the interview in his *Songs of Scotland,* 1849-50.

QUESTION 235
What connection did Burns have with the famous "Allan Line" of Trans-Atlantic Liners?

Answer
The line was formed by his cousin, Alexander Allan. The Allan family of
"Old Rome" near Gatehead, Kilmarnock, were related through Burns'
mother. The third son of Jean and James Allan, Alexander learnt the
trade of shoe-making in Kilmarnock, went into ships' carpentry and
took up a seafaring life. He eventually founded the "Allan Line"
(Glasgow and Liverpool) and died in 1854, aged 74.

QUESTION 236
When did Burns last spell his name "Burness"?

Answer
3rd April, 1786. On this date Burns wrote two surviving letters – the first
to Robert Aiken of Ayr, signed Burness; the second to Gavin Hamilton
of Mauchline Castle, signed Burns. There were different spellings of the
name – Burns, Burnes, Burness. Spelling was not standardised in Burns'
day.

QUESTION 237
What did the young Burns threaten to do with a copy of *Titus
Andronicus*?

Answer
Burn it.
   When he read it as a young boy at Alloway, the story horrified him
with its cruelty. John Murdoch read the story to the assembled family.

QUESTION 238
What was the *London Star* hoax?

Answer
A faked report in the newspaper by Henry Dundas, later Viscount
Melville, in which the Duchess of Gordon was insultingly described and
Burns falsely accused of the charge.
   The Duchess was a forthright person who made enemies. She told Sir
Walter Scott, however, that Robert Burns was the only man whose
conversation had swept her off her feet. Burns' attention was drawn to
"sneering verses about the duchess and reputed to be by him".
   On 10th April, 1789, he wrote to the *London Star* objecting to the piece
and rejecting responsibility.

QUESTION 239
The *First Statistical Account of Scotland* is a unique and important book
the world over. What part did Burns take in it?

Answer

He wrote about the Monkland Friendly Society, a library founded by Burns and his neighbour, Captain Robert Riddell.

The statistical Accounts of Scotland were unique in their genre. The first was published in 1792. Monkland is in Dunscore Parish, Nithsdale and Burns was, in that autumn of 1791, in Ellisland. His neighbour was Captain Robert Riddell of Friars Carse. Burns supplied the inspiration and Riddell the subscribers to form the Monklands Friendly Society, "To store the minds of the lower classes with useful knowledge".

QUESTION 240

When Burns had his seal designed he was most emphatic about a particular part of the design. Which part was it?

Answer

The holly must be a holly bush and not a holly tree.

Why Burns should have chosen holly for his real design is hard to define. One theory is that it was intended as a compliment to his mother, Agnes Brown, or it was because her father had been a forester on the Culzean estate, and Culzean meant "The place of Holly", or it could have been Burns' regard for the holly tree.

QUESTION 241

What action did Burns take to show his sympathy during the French Revolution?

Answer

Bought four carronades to send to the French Convention.

It is believed Burns bought these carronades at a sale for four pounds, but according to the Train Manuscripts, Sir Walter Scott tried unsuccessfully to trace the receipts of the guns in France, and thereafter applied to the Custom House Authorities, who claimed that they had been seized at the Port of Dover. Further research was made upon the matter but nothing concrete ever came to light, though in view of the proven accuracy of the rest of Train's claim, it would be rash to assume the carronades were never despatched.

QUESTION 242

Burns, along with Gilbert, received an award of three pounds in 1783. In what capacity did they receive it?

Answer

Their reward from an agricultural body for improving the strain of flax seed.

Many critics of Burns have labelled him as a poor farmer, but this belief does not hold according to Colonel William Fullerton, who wrote a *Review on Agriculture in the County of Ayr.* In his review, which was published in 1793, he spoke of the dangers arising from horned cattle, and the correct methods to be undertaken as suggested to him by Burns.

QUESTION 243
How old was Burns when he wrote "O Tibbie I hae Seen The Day"?

Answer
About seventeen years of age.

Mrs Begg, Burns' sister, identified this poem with Isabella Stevenson of Little Hill, by Locklea. At that time Burns was the leading labourer at Lochlea Farm.

QUESTION 244
In which year was the first Edinburgh edition printed?

Answer
1787.

The first Edinburgh Edition of Burns' poems was published by William Creech, on the 21st April, 1787. It was dedicated to the Noblemen and gentlemen of the Caledonian Hunt and there were one thousand five hundred subscribers, who called for two thousand eight hundred copies.

QUESTION 245
In which year did Robert and Gilbert take over Mossgiel Farm?

Answer
March, 1784.

Mossgiel (old spelling Mossgaville), is in the parish of Mauchline, three miles from Lochlea, has a little over one hundred acres and the Burns family paid Mr Hamilton an annual rental of ninety pounds. It was a joint concern, every member of the family received a wage for the labour he performed on the farm. Robert and Gilbert's allowance was seven pounds per annum each.

Burns wrote many of his fine works at Mossgiel, including "The Address to the Deil", "The Holy Fair", "Death and Dr Hornbook", "The Twa Dogs", "The lass of Ballochmyle", "The Cottar's Saturday Night" and several others.

QUESTION 246
For how many years did Burns hold the position as deputy master in the

masons of St James' Lodge, Tarbolton, which became separated again from St David's Lodge?

Answer

Four.

Burns was a mason until his death and was initiated on the 4th July, 1781 in St David's Lodge No. 174 at Tarbolton, was passed and raised in the same Lodge on the 1st October, 1781 and on his visit to Edinburgh was made a member of Canongate Kilwinning Lodge No. 2. Burns received honorary membership from Loudon Kilwinning at Newmilns, on 27th March, 1786 and from St John's Kilwinning, Kilmarnock on 26th October, 1786. He moved to Dumfries 27th December, 1791 and became a member of St Andrew's Lodge No. 176 and was elected senior warden in 1792.

QUESTION 247

Burns made a prophecy to his wife which proved true. What was it?

Answer

"I shall be more respected a hundred years after I am dead than I am at present".

After a brief illness – made briefer at the thought of leaving his wife and family unprovided – Burns said the above lines. True prophet, no less than true poet.

QUESTION 248

When was the Bachelors' Club at Tarbolton founded?

Answer

November, 1780.

This debating club was founded on the 22nd November, 1780 by Robert and Gilbert Burns along with Hugh Reid, Alexander Brown, Thomas Wright, William McGavin and Walter Mitchell. The first meeting was held in the home of John Richard and Burns was elected president for the night. David Sillar later became a member and the building is now a museum.

QUESTION 249

What was the maiden name of Burns' mother?

Answer

Agnes Brown.

She was the daughter of Gilbert Brown, a tenant of a three hundred acre farm on Craigenton, Kirkoswald and was the eldest of six children.

She was only ten years old when her mother died, and she took care of the family for two years, until her father remarried. She was then sent to stay with her grandmother at Maybole.

She met her husband William Burnes, at the Maybole Fair in 1756 and was married on the 15th December, 1757. Maybole at that time, was the stronghold of the Kennedy family. Mrs Burnes bore her first child, Robert, when she was twenty seven years old, and gave birth to a further six children. William Burnes died in 1784, and she died thirty six years later. Her latter years were spent living at Gilbert's house, Grant's Braes, East Lothian and she is buried in the churchyard at Bolton. Mrs Begg, Burns' sister, said of her mother, "she possessed a fine musical ear and sang well".

QUESTION 250
Burns wrote on the 24th February to his friend Ballantine: "I am getting my phiz done by an eminent engraver". Who was the engraver?

Answer
John Buego.

Buego, born in Edinburgh in 1759, was an apprentice engraver, later setting up a business for himself. He met Burns when Creech employed him to engrave the Nasmyth portrait for the second edition of Burns' poems, known as the First Edinburgh Edition. He continued in his letter, "If it can be ready in time I will appear in my book, looking like all other fools, to my title page".

Buego married Elizabeth McDowall of Edinburgh, by whom he had a daughter. He died in 1841 and was buried in Greyfriars Churchyard.

SECTION 6

QUESTION 251
Where in the United States can a replica of Burns' cottage be seen?

Answer
In Atlanta, Georgia.

The Burns Club of Atlanta purchased land in 1907 and built a replica of the birthplace of Burns. Mr Thomas Morgan made the plans and Mr R. McWhirter supervised the building. The cottage is of granite with a corrugated iron roof.

QUESTION 252
Which statue of Burns has an amusing but ill-founded situation?

Answer

The statue of Burns in Denedin, New Zealand, is so placed that Burns appears to have turned his back on St Paul's Cathedral but faces the Oban Hotel. The statue was unveiled on Queen Victoria's birthday on 24th May, 1887.

QUESTION 253

Which admirer of Burns was descended from the Scottish patriot, King Robert the Bruce?

Answer

Mrs Catherine Bruce ("Lady Clackmannan").

Mrs Bruce was a Jacobite and the sword used was reported to be the two-handed sword of King Robert the Bruce (*see* Question 219)

QUESTION 254

Why should Burnsians the world over be indebted to Colonel John Gribbel?

Answer

When to their shame the Liverpool Athenaeum decided to sell the Burns' manuscripts, which Currie had given them to the exclusion of the Burns family, Colonel Gribbel of Philadelphia bought them in the U.S.A. in June 1913 and presented them to the Scottish people.

QUESTION 255

Who wrote (a) the words; and (b) the music for "The Star O'Rabbie Burns"?

Answer

(a) James Thomson of Hawick Burns Club.
(b) James Booth. Date unknown – Thomson was the first president of the Hawick Burns Club in 1878.

QUESTION 256

What became of Burns' House, Dumfries, after the death of Jean Armour Burns?

Answer

In 1851 Colonel William Nicol Burns purchased it; in 1885 he gave it to the Dumfries and Maxwelltown Educational Society to be used for poor and needy boys.

QUESTION 257

Why were the early Burns' Suppers celebrated each year on 29th January?

86

Answer
Despite Burns' song "Rantin' Rovin' Robin" which mentioned 25th January as his birth date, Currie for some reason stated the 29th to be the day of his birth.

QUESTION 258
Who gave the famous Nasmyth portrait of Burns to the nation?

Answer
Colonel William Nicol Burns, the son of the poet, donated the painting which is now in the Scottish National Portrait Galley, Edinburgh.

QUESTION 259
Did Sir Henry Raeburn paint Burns' portrait?

Answer
Raeburn did not paint a portrait of Burns.

He did however, make a copy of the Nasmyth painting for the 1808 proposed edition of the poems by Cadell & Davies, London. He was paid 20 guineas but the copy was never used and has disappeared. Raeburn still ranks as the greatest Scottish portrait painter. Had he painted Burns from life he would have painted "warts and all" and killed all subsequent argument as to what Burns really looked like.

QUESTION 260
Where is the Coull Anderson Library of Burns Genealogy?

Answer
Dewar House, Hill Terrace, Arbroath.

Mr Coull Anderson, a native of the United States and a Burns Family descendant, bequeathed his estate in 1970 to the establishment for Burns family genealogy.

QUESTION 261
Name any hospital containing a memorial to Burns in the form of an endowed bed or such accommodation?

Answer
One of the following: Aberdeen, Birmingham, Derby, Edinburgh, Greenock, Liverpool and Londonderry.

Feelings ran that hospital beds and accommodation for old people served as more useful memorials than statues.

QUESTION 262
Where are the headquarters of the Burns Federation?

Answer
The Dick Institute, Kilmarnock, Ayrshire.

QUESTION 263
The Burns Federation failed to get a Chair of Scottish Literature introduced to a Scottish university. In what way, however, did they succeed?

Answer
At the beginning of the 20th century, Scottish universities ignored
Scottish history and literature. The Federation succeeded in getting
Glasgow University to set up the Chair of History in 1915.

QUESTION 264
Which Burns club secretary was fined for using headed notepaper
bearing the Burns coat-of-arms?

Answer
Henry Flockhart, secretary of the Hawick Burns Club, was fined
£2.2.0d in 1898 for this infringement.

QUESTION 265
Why should Burnsians not recite the poem beginning "My Lord, I
would not fill your chair. . ."?

Answer
Because the author was not Burns. These lines are typical of later
compositions which would place Burns in a class struggle.

It was another example of the brash attempt to illustrate Burns as a
fighter for social equality – than which nothing was farther from the
truth. The *Burns Chronicles* right say that, at the least, such poems
show Burns to have an extremely high opinion of himself.

QUESTION 266
When was the Burns Federation instituted?

Answer
1885.

After the dedication service at Westminster Abbey, London, for the
memorial to Robert Burns in Poets' Corner, the Provost of Kilmarnock,
David Mackay, suggested that a world wide organisation of Burns
Clubs would be appropriate. A meeting was then called in Kilmarnock
and the Burns Federation instituted.

QUESTION 267
Name the first ladies Burns Club and when it was formed.

Answer
Shotts, Lanarkshire in 1920.

QUESTION 268
Which is the earliest overseas club to join the Burns Federation?

Answer
Dunedin Burns Club, New Zealand, formed in 1861 and joined the Federation in 1894.

The publication of the *Burns Chronicle* starting in 1892, has encouraged many overseas clubs.

QUESTION 269
Next to which poet's memorial is Burns' bust in Poets' Corner in Westminster Abbey?

Answer
William Shakespeare.

QUESTION 270
Which Royal personage headed one of the "Shilling Subscription" lists for a memorial to Burns in Westminster Abbey in 1884-5?

Answer
The Prince of Wales, later King Edward VII.

QUESTION 271
Is there a Robert Burns tartan?

Answer
Marchand.

There is the Robert Burns check which was produced by Baron March and of Messrs. George Harrison & Co. of Edinburgh. It is now sold throughout Scotland.

QUESTION 272
How much did the Royal Literary Fund donate to Burns' widow and family?

Answer
£25 in 1796; £20 in 1801. The Royal Literary Fund, still extant, was a benevolent society for the relief of poverty for authors and their families.

QUESTION 273
What especial claim is made by Dalry, Ayrshire, Burns Club?

89

Answer

The longest unbroken sequence of anniversary celebrations from 1826.

QUESTION 274

"Twas then a blast O' Janwar win
Blew hansel in on Robin"

What does this mean?

Answer

When Burns was a few days old, a wind storm blew down part of the Alloway Cottage and Mrs Burns and baby Robert had to seek temporary shelter with neighbours.

QUESTION 275

What role did the Incorporation of Shoemakers of Ayr play in the Burns' story?

Answer

They purchased Burns Cottage from William Burnes for £160 in 1781; after renting it out for a variety of tenants and reasons, they sold it to Cottage trustees for £4,000 in 1881.

QUESTION 276

When and where was the first Burns' Supper held?

Answer

Summer, 1801, Alloway.

The Rev Hamilton Paul left an account of the first Burns' Supper. He and eight others met in the cottage and resolved to celebrate the next supper on 29th January, 1802 – the date stupidly misinterpreted by Currie. Of the nine, two of Burns friends were present, Robert Aiken ("Orator Bob") and John Ballantine, Provost of Ayr. The Rev Paul left reports on these suppers up to 1810.

QUESTION 277

Name two theatrical productions based on the life of Burns.

Answer

Drinkwater's *Robert Burns*, 1925; Storm's *Three Goose Quills and a Knife*, 1967; Stirling's *Scotland's Sons*, 1945-1955; Wright's *There was a Lad*, 1968; Lee's *Robert Burns*, 1926 or Crozier's *Rab the Rhymer*, 1953.

QUESTION 278

What was the "Temple Hoax"?

Answer

Andrew Carnegie was upset at a ceremony when delicately asked to be a benefactor in general. As a reaction a local magistrate began a hoax that Carnegie had given £500,000 for a Burns Temple in Kilmarnock.

The ceremony was connected with Carnegie's educational interests and was held in Kilmarnock. The ethical reaction to the hoax was that the Kilmarnock Burns Club, from public appeals and contributions, had the memorial tower and statue built in Kay Park, near the town centre.

QUESTION 279

Burns occasionally writes of "begging", what does he mean?

Answer

Not begging in the modern sense. Rather the use of his gift of poetry, song and debate to entertain – as with the medieval troubador. Such "begging" or sale of talents was on a much higher level than the lines illustrated in *The Jolly Beggars*.

QUESTION 280

Although Burns visited the club, but makes no reference to playing the game, why should he be indebted to Kilmarnock Bowling Club?

Answer

According to Paterson, the historian of Ayrshire, its members stood as guarantors for the First Edition of his poetry.

John Goldie, a wine merchant and author, was impressed by Burns' literary prowess, and after visiting him at harvest-time in 1785 at Lochlea, he asked Burns to come to his house, "take pot luck" as to dinner, then meet with and read some of his works, to some of his friends. According to Paterson the result was the first, or Kilmarnock, edition of Burns' poetry.

QUESTION 281

On arriving at Dumfries for Burns' funeral how much was brother Gilbert able to give Jean Armour to buy food?

Answer

One shilling.

The emotional incident in James Barke's novel is confirmed in the account book of Gilbert Burns now in Kilmarnock. Gilbert raised eleven children, so never had much money.

QUESTION 282

Give the meaning of the motto "Better a wee bush than nae bield" in Burns' proposed coat-of-arms?

Answer

"Better a small bush than no shelter".

QUESTION 283

"My tocher's the jewel has charm for him". What was "tocher"?

Answer

Dowry, given as part of a wedding arrangement.

The poem "My tocher's the jewel", to the music of "Lord Elcho's Favourite", was highly thought of by Burns.

QUESTION 284

What is a "cutty sark"?

Answer

A short shirt or part of underwear.

The wearing of such an abbreviated form of dress by one of the witches in the poem "Tam O'Shanter" would allow her physical charms to be easily seen.

QUESTION 285

What was the "Letter from Hell"?

Answer

Burns' letter to Maria Riddell following the "Rape of the Sabines" incident at Friars' Carse.

After-dinner drinking influenced Robert Riddell's fellow guests to burst in upon the ladies and feign an attack on them. Later evidence by servants stated that Burns had tried to stop the nonsense, had been taunted by the other men and consequently led the attack. Riddell's wife objected and Burns was made the scapegoat.

QUESTION 286

When did the brew house at Ayr take the name of the Tam O'Shanter Inn?

Answer

1842.

The starting point of "Tam O'Shanter's" famous ride was the brew house owned by Benjamin Graham, a cousin of Douglas Graham, of

"Tam O'Shanter" fame. The brewer and his wife acted the parts of landlord and landlady in the poem.

QUESTION 287
What were Sowans?

Answer
Soured "seconds" of oatmeal eaten in milk. The staple diet in Burns' day among the poorer classes.

QUESTION 288
What was a "cutty stool"?

Answer
A stool of repentance on which sinners publicly knelt for confession and punishment for some or other moral lapse.

Burns was obliged to sit on the stool of repentance in full view of the assembled church congregation in Mauchline for his over-ardent courtship with Jean Armour.

QUESTION 289
What is the reputed connection between Burns and the South American word "gringo"?

Answer
Tradition has it that American army personnel favoured Burns' "Green Grow the Rashes" and from that the white troops were referred to as "gringos". The term is abusive and refers especially to Americans and Englishmen.

QUESTION 290
Name the best known authors of books on Burns written by (a) a German and (b) a Frenchman.

Answer
(a) Hans Hecht (b) Auguste Angellier.

QUESTION 291
What "international incident" arose regarding the Burns Federation pocket diplomas of membership?

Answer
In 1965 a number of Pakistani immigrants produced copies of the pocket diplomas as proof of residence in the United Kingdom. The Burns Federation pocket diploma was, to put it politely, not recognised

by the Immigration Authorities at Prestwick Airport as being valid passports.

QUESTION 292
Name three outstanding collections or libraries of Burns' works and manuscripts in Scotland.

Answer
Mitchell Library, Glasgow; Edinburgh University; Burns Cottage, Alloway; Irvine Burns Club; Burns Monument; Kilmarnock and Ayr, Dumfries, Dunfermline and Kilmarnock Public Libraries.

QUESTION 293
A recent valuation of an original manuscript of "Tam O'Shanter" was £25,000. How much did Burns earn for writing it?

Answer
Nothing, he wrote it for Capt. Francis Grose.
Burns was against making money from his god-given gift of poetry. Apart from the sale of his Kilmarnock and Edinburgh Editions and an argument over £5 with Thomson, the Edinburgh publisher, he took no money for his work. He even declined an income from journalism.

QUESTION 294
Apart from the first Edinburgh Edition of Burns' poetry, what other work of world note did William Smellie edit and print?

Answer
The first edition of the *Encyclopaedia Britannica* published in Edinburgh in 1768.

QUESTION 295
What did James Veitch, editor of *Burns Chronicle*, consider to be the best biography of Burns?

Answer
The Life of Robert Burns by Professor Franklyn B. Snyder.
Snyder was Professor of North Western University, Illinois. Unusually with a writer on the poet, he is clear-headed and not subjective. Would that other biographers were as free from emotion and prejudice as he.

QUESTION 296
How would one immediately recognise a Kilmarnock First Edition or an absolute facsimile of it?

94

Answer

The title-page has two obvious errors – after "Poems" the comma is placed above the true line and at the bottom inner border the vertical rule or line is missing on the right.

QUESTION 297

What is a "Hornbook"?

Answer

A child's alphabet etc. covered with a thin sheet of transparent horn to preserve the paper. Burns use of the term "Dr Hornbook" gave a hint of the identity of the hero of the poem – John Wilson, the Tarbolton school master.

QUESTION 298

Name (a) the first, and (b) the greatest Russian translators of the poetry of Burns?

Answer

(a) Lermontov   (b) Marshak.

The poets represent the beginnings and high points in Russian translations. Lermontov was the descendant of the Scot, Capt. George Learmont, a mercenary in the Russian armed forces.

Marshak has done more than any Russian to publicise in that country the works of Burns. It is interesting to add that Burns' songs and epitaphs are the most acceptable forms of works matching Russian tastes.

QUESTION 299

In 1791 Burns surrendered the lease at Ellisland Farm to Mr Miller and removed his family to the town of Dumfries. How many children did he take with him? Give name and age.

Answer

Three.

Robert named after the poet, aged five years.

Francis Wallace named after Mrs Dunlop of Dunlop, aged two years.

William Nicol named after William Nicol of the High School, Edinburgh, aged one year.

Jean Armour had a further three children whilst living in Dumfries. Elizabeth Riddell in 1792 who died at a very early age and was named after Mrs Robert Riddell of Glenriddell, James Glencairn in 1794 named after the Earl of Glencairn and Maxwell named after Dr Maxwell was born on the day of the poet's funeral.

QUESTION 300

Burns was well aware his days were numbered. From which of his letters do we draw this conclusion?

Answer

On July 7th, 1796 (a fortnight before his death) he is writing his friend Cunningham, "I fear the voice of the Bard will soon be heard among you no more". About the same date he is writing his wife, addressing her as "My dearest Love", and to his brother Gilbert he writes, "I am dangerously ill and not likely to get better. God keep my wife and children". On the 21st July, Burns died. His kinsman Carlyle has written:

"And thus he passed, not softly, yet speedily, into that still country, where the hail storms and fire-showers do not reach, and the heaviest laden wayfarer at length lays down his load."